Hyper to Holy

How Jesus
Touched the Life of a Housewife
AN AUTOBIOGRAPHY

Third Printing

Gwen Mouliert

KeeperPublishing

Hyper to Holy

How Jesus
Touched The Life of a Housewife
AN AUTOBIOGRAPHY

ISBN: 978-0-615-41255-9

Copyright © 1990
All Rights Reserved

Gwen Mouliert

Cover design by KeeperGraphics CS,
www.KeeperGraphics.com

KeeperPublishing and KeeperGraphics are part of
Gervaro Enterprises, LLC., located in northern New Jersey.

Published by KeeperPublishing
Gervaro Enterprises, LLC.
PO Box 175,
Swartswood, NJ 07877
rgervasi@gervaroenterprises.com

Printed in United States of America.

Contents

Dedication

To my husband, who has stuck by me through
thick and thin, or should I say, through
fat and thin.

To my children, who have eaten thin
hamburger patties for seven days in
a row so I could write.

To Aileen Pandapas, God's executive secretary,
and my dear friend.

This is beginning to sound like the
Academy Awards so I would just say,
in Jesus' Name . . . Thanks!

Introduction

In most Christian books the introduction is done by a well-known person: Pat Boone, Oral Roberts, or maybe Pat Robertson would have been nice. The problem is that these people don't know me, but then again, neither do you — which is one reason I am about to write my own life story — introduction and all.

I will be sharing with you my joys and sorrows in honesty and in truth. For such a long time I was sure someone with a degree (journalism would have been very nice) would be writing this for me. Even now I fight the urge to run off to college or at least to do a correspondence course of study of the Bible through the mail.

I felt that if I penned this, it might end up required reading in a pre-school somewhere. I am thankful the Lord reminded me of I Corinthians 2:1: "And I, brethren, when I came to you, came not with excellency of speech or of wisdom, declaring unto you the testimony of God."

As you prepare to read my testimony of what great things God has done for me, you may not feel the need for "Webster's" dictionary, but I pray you will feel the need for more of Jesus.

CHAPTER I.

Oh My, A Pink Elephant!

I can't start this book with "in the beginning" or even "Once upon a time." I will share, however, with you how I know now is the time for me to write this book.

The Lord has allowed me to speak in many different churches and to various ladies groups the past few years and on many occasions I have been asked if I have written a book. Even my pastor had encouraged me some years ago to start a diary because he felt I would one day write a book.

Little did he know that I had begun to keep a diary six months prior to his suggestion. Be assured that my pastor did not miss God's timing. It has been true in my life that after the Lord speaks to me, He is kind enough many times to confirm what He has said through someone else. Haven't you found that to be true in your own life?

What finally got my pen to paper was an incident which occurred while I was on Jury Duty. There was a great deal of free time, and I saw this as an opportunity to serve my country as well as my God. I began to pray for an opening to be a witness — not for the State, you understand, but for the Lord Jesus.

On one particular day we had to be available all day on call, yet there was no need for us to serve. The Lord brought a delightful young (now that I am in my early thirties anyone under forty is young) girl, Jennifer, into my life. As I began to share with her parts of my personal testimony, her response after each phrase was laughter mixed with words such as: "I know you read this in a book!" — "Come on, child, you wrote a book!" — "Honey, this ought to be in print." Well, I knew that many believers had been asking me to share my story in a book, but now God was speaking to me through a non-believer. I wasn't going to wait for a donkey to speak to me on the road somewhere, so now . . .

"In the beginning" I was born in Atlantic City in the summer of '47. Sounds like a movie title, doesn't it? I was the middle child (and only daughter) born to George and Helen Prague.

As a little girl I remember my Mommy was sick a great deal of the time. When I was just a small child, my Father would take me over to Ohio Avenue and Pacific Avenue and I would stand on the corner holding his hand so very tightly, while from a high balcony window a woman in a wheelchair would be waving at me and throwing kisses. It was, of course, my Mom in the hospital. I wanted so to be on her lap, and I would think it must be fun to be so high up and watch all the cars go by. This soon became a habit, however, every weekend just standing there, looking up, waving and crying. I soon realized crying wouldn't bring her down to me and so with each hospital admittance and with every operation, I hardened by heart because of the pain involved. I loved my Mommy so — closing myself off was the only way I knew to handle the situation.

My Daddy was sorry. All their friends were sorry. My relatives were all sorry, but no one could bring her down to me. There I was — this little girl — on a big street corner waving at a lady high up who I just didn't know anymore.

The operations finally stopped and my Mother was home. Our home was now in a little town called Pleasantville, New Jersey, only a short distance from the shore. Life was pleasant those early years, and my younger brother, Ronnie, was born.

My older brother, Dirk, really helped to make those years fun for me. He convinced me that his friend had a real, honest-to-goodness space ship and that on Saturdays they would go to the man on the moon and they'd send us something back to prove they really went. Every Saturday morning my brother Ronnie and I would stand next to this huge oak tree in our yard with our little eyes closed ... waiting ... and sure enough, from the sky would fall our favorite candy — right there in New Jersey. I don't know how long my big brother hung out over the roof like that, but I'll thank him always. When I did find out, it was such a heartbreaker! We could handle no Easter Bunny and even no Santa, 'cause those fellows only happen once a year, but we had a good thing going every Saturday morning.

During those early years when Mom was home, I couldn't have been any happier. Then, once again, sickness hit our happy family. This time it was something to affect us all. My mother awoke one morning to find herself paralyzed. The ambulance came — it was as if panic hit our home. The house was always full of people trying to help, and I can now thank God for them, but to a girl six years old and already frightened, all the noise and confusion increased my fears.

For many, many months my mother was in this bedridden condition. The three of us were then eleven, six, and three years of age, and fighting and crying most of the time. My folks had some dear friends who were trying to take care of us, but I didn't want someone else cooking for and feeding me. I remember well the nights we couldn't find someone to cook for us. Daddy had only two entrees: codfish cakes or hot dogs split and fried until they became a bridge over our instant potatoes — we would have war games at supper. This may seem silly to you, but it was my Dad's way of holding his family together.

After eight months, which to me seemed like eight years, Mom had surgery and was learning to walk again. All that time I felt I was the woman of the house. As Mom was now able to do more and more for us, I felt like she was taking Dad away from me. I didn't know how to keep his attention, so I began to overeat.

I became a fat little girl at age ten or so. Everyone kept telling me it was a baby fat — no need to fear. Dad would kid that I could outeat any truck driver he knew. As the years added, so did the pounds. Once Daddy took us to a Union picnic where I ate two whole blueberry pies and won the contest. But, inside, I felt like such a loser. My increasing weight problem caused severe trouble between Mom and me. I was now attending a Catholic school and because of my size, I had to have a special uniform made to fit me. This became the joke of the school. For many years it seemed someone was always making fun of my size.

My mother tried every way she knew to help me lose weight. We tried the hard-boiled egg diet, the grapefruit diet, the "Metri-call" diet, etc. All the while I was approaching neighbors saying that my mother sent me over for cookies. I would eat the whole bag of cookies each time. I was chunky and had rosy cheeks which matched my bottom when all of the neighbors came to collect their groceries!

When the kids at school would make fun of me or call me

names, I would just go home and eat all the more. I would prove to them I was not a "fat slob."

Easter was the one holiday I dreaded because it meant a new outfit. Oh, I was thrilled about the hat, gloves, and shoes, but when it came to a dress, we headed to the Chubbett's. There were only one or two different styles and all the while it cost my folks extra. I felt bad about that so I'd eat some more and after a few bowls of ice cream, I would feel better and the outfit didn't look so bad then and I would forget the price.

I was not very popular those early school years even though I tried to be nice. I was always being laughed at so I became a clown, but inside there was no laughter.

Upon entering high school, I was almost 200 pounds. My self-image was very poor, and as the jokes about my size increased, the hardness and wall I was building around me for protection became unbreakable. You couldn't get to me now no matter what you said or did!

I remember when my next door neighbor won a horse in a contest. The whole block was so excited, just waiting for the day the horse was to come. I got up very early and watched out the window of my bedroom. Before I could even get dressed, the kids were lined up three-deep. I, too, waited in line as her father would walk each child around the yard for a ride. The joy and thrill was on each face as they pretended to be Sally Starr — at least, the girls did. Now, my turn! As I approached the horse, this girl's father told me I was too fat to ride and I would break the horse's back. The kids got hysterical over that one, and I ran home in tears once again.

I am sure this hurt my mother. Try as she may, I only ate more and more. No sweetheart dances or proms for me. The only boys who knew me by name were those who worked at the "Dairy Queen" at the corner for the summer.

I never felt that I fitted in. At this point my Dad was working a good many hours to pay off all the medical expenses that had accumulated over the years. My big brother, Dirk, was now in the Navy and away from home.

It was at this point Mother thought maybe she could get me to wake up and see that I was ruining my life. She kept telling me to look at myself — that I was becoming a fat slob and no man was ever going to love me. I know with all my heart she didn't mean that and only said it to try to help me see what I was doing to myself. But I did feel all those things already deep within myself.

Just once I wanted to be a part of the crowd. In my senior year the mohair sweaters became very popular. I begged and pleaded until Mother said I could have one. We spent the entire day shopping because this sweater had to be perfect. We finally found it — a size 44 light pink mohair sweater. Not only did I get a sweater, but a new white blouse with a Peter Pan collar and a pink wool skirt. I could hardly wait for Monday to go to school. I was so proud and pleased and so thankful to Mom for making this day possible.

As I walked into the first period class, "Family Living," one of the boys shouted, "Oh my God, it's a pink elephant!"

I didn't wear my pink sweater for graduation, but I did graduate from high school in 1965.

CHAPTER II

Who Would Marry a Boo Boo?

As I was rushing off to work a little late one morning, I glanced in the full-length mirror in our hallway upstairs. That mirror had been there for as long as I can remember, but this was indeed the first time I really saw myself. Baby, my "baby fat" they kept telling me about was all grown up — hanging on for dear life. Right then I set my mind to lose weight because I knew I wouldn't find a man in the shape I was in.

Women didn't pursue careers in the sixties as they do now. The one thing a girl did when she got out of high school was to go get a man. I decided it was time to go husband-hunting!

I was then working with a gal named Michelle who wanted me to move in with her and her daughter in their apartment. I thought this would really be the life. I was now working two full-time jobs. After "Two Guys" all day, I would jump in the shower and then go off to the diner for the four to twelve shift.

I was so busy with this schedule, I only ate one meal a day and soon lost 85 pounds. For the very first time I was thin like everyone else. The only problem was that I stayed fat in my head for such a long, long time. At 18½ I moved in with Michelle. I know this hurt my parents, but I felt like I had to find myself — or so they say. Who are **they** anyway?

The arrangement worked out was for me to give Michelle a certain amount of money every payday to cover my share of the bills. After a few months I invited Mom and Dad to dinner. I was so proud to be entertaining my first dinner guests. I came home to get ready to cook a meal that would put Julia Childs to shame only to find out that our electricity was disconnected because our bills hadn't been paid in months. At the door appear the proud parents of a girl who is smiling at them and in her heart is preparing Michelle's funeral.

I talked my parents into eating subs by candlelight, with one excuse or another, soft music playing in the background. Our landlord starts to bang on our door at this point, shouting that our rent is long overdue and he is not going to have deadbeats around.

There's no place like home. That's where I went. That's where I belonged.

I was beginning to date as many men as possible. I felt like I had years to make up, and it was now my turn to hurt people. As soon as I felt anyone becoming serious, I would drop him.

I was looking for a man to sweep me off my feet. I was now thin and around five foot seven. I figured I'd better survey some basketball players. The man of my dreams would be at least seven feet tall, have a 48-inch chest and a 29-inch waist.

My girlfriend Viki kept telling me I needed to meet her brother. His name is Concepcion, but everyone calls him Boo Boo. Makes sense, right?

During my days away from home with Michelle, Boo had written to me a few times from where he was fighting in Viet Nam while in the Army. He had only seen me once or twice previous to this time and he had no idea that I was thin now. Viki was working on him, too. I think we just wrote each other to be nice and to keep peace with Viki.

One summer evening while riding through Atlantic City on the back of two motorcycles with our dates, a girlfriend and I saw Viki ahead of us in her brother's red Comet. (Viki was taking care of his car while he was overseas.) We chased the car, calling for Viki. When we caught up to the car, we found out, much to our surprise and embarrassment, it contained Boo Boo and his buddy, Charlie Brown (real name, honest). They had the nerve, in front of these leather-jacket dates of ours, to ask my girlfriend and me to join them for dinner. Well, we did!

Viki was so right; her brother was all she said he was. The only thing she never mentioned was his size. He wasn't fat — just short, and noticeably shorter than I. I cared for him right away and was angry at myself. I felt I had been laughed at all my life and if I went with him, there would be even more laughter. If I were to wear heels, it was Mutt 'n Jeff for sure. Why was it that what other people thought was so very important? I was looking for a tall Mr. Atlas to carry on my arm through town to show them. Here I had been dating a few tall and handsome young men, but try as I may, I just didn't feel anything for them at all. Now, in just one night over tuna salad sandwiches, looking in Boo Boo's brown eyes, I hoped I would see him again.

I didn't even mention him or the dinner to my folks when I got home because there was a problem much deeper than elevator shoes could fix. Boo was a non-Catholic. He was a Protestant! I was raised in a strict Roman Catholic home. Even in my childhood years I was not to play with Protestants, and I was taught that no matter what, you don't go into their churches.

Three of my mother's sisters are nuns, and they spent many vacations in the summers with us. All I knew was that if you were a Protestant, you were someone who was protesting the Catholic faith. I know this is not true, but at this time in my life, I believed it.

In a day or so, Boo asked me to go to the drive-in with him. I went gladly. If I didn't sit up too straight, no one would know our problem. That night was the best date I ever had. Boo was so much fun to be with. I eased into a conversation about religion only to discover Boo was a Pentecostal!

My knowledge of Pentecost was that it had several Sundays named after it. During Mass each Sunday I would hear: First Sunday after Pentecost, Second Sunday after Pentecost, and so on, but I never knew nor understood what Pentecost was. As I look back now, it's a good thing.

I never dated anyone else again. I just knew deep inside this Boo Boo was for me. In no time at all we were going steady and after six months, he asked me to marry him. When I realized how serious he was, I felt it was now time for him to convert to Catholicism.

Christmas Eve in 1967 we went to Midnight Mass together. It was still in Latin. Boo had never been in a Catholic church and he kept poking me to ask me what the priest was saying. I was afraid that at any moment God was going to strike him down dead for irreverence. At this point lightning through the ceiling was my only concern. We never even spoke in church, let alone questioned what Father was saying.

Once outside, Boo wanted me to translate the Mass in Latin into English for him. When I told him I didn't know Latin, he wanted to know why I went there. (My dear Catholic believers: Please don't become offended. You really need to finish this book to get your money's worth.)

I know that Jesus was there in my church whether Latin or English was spoken. Jesus is wherever there is someone with a heart towards God. I think all those years I went to church out of a sense of duty, obligation, and the fear of God. At this point Boo said he would take instructions so we could be married by a priest in the Catholic church, but he would not convert.

I would not even consider going to his church, and it was apparent he wasn't going to go with me every Sunday. I then made a mistake that later had a real effect on my life. I stopped going to church at all. For the first time I didn't feel as though I needed God. I was thin now, had a good job, a little money in the bank, and someone who said he loved me. Inside I still had a very hard time believing he could really love me or that any man would really love me. I kept thinking that when he really got to know me, he would stop loving me. You see, I didn't love myself at all — it didn't matter if I wore a size 10 or not. All those years of being fat had left me very insecure and looking for love, but not able to receive it. I knew I loved him, but would or could he grow at 23?

At this point in our lives, without God, we made plans for our future. We would be married — wait two years — and have our first child — then, after two more years, have our second child.

My parents gave us a beautiful wedding early in 1968. We were married in the Catholic Church of Assumption. I never would have made it down that aisle without my Daddy. There we were, arm-in-arm, the wedding march ringing out from the organ, 120 people staring at me, and my father begins to tell me how he has waited twenty years for this and now his food bill should drop by hundreds of dollars each month.

One of the most touching moments of that day came when I danced with my father at the reception to the tune of "Daddy's Little Girl." We were both in tears that afternoon. When the song ended, I ran to the Ladies' Room in sobs. I couldn't even get in to get a tissue for all the women crying in line ahead of me.

Now, as Mrs. Mouliert, my husband and I were going to fly down to Puerto Rico for a week's honeymoon. I had never been in a jet, but I knew it would be all right because my Boo Boo was there with me. As we boarded the plane, being married

15

only a few hours, my husband handed our tickets to the stewardess, and she separated us. I couldn't believe this was happening. What about " 'til death do us part"? Was this to be my only flight?

They placed me next to an older gentleman, with Boo about four rows away on the aisle. Even if we'd been separated across from one another on the aisle, I could have handled it — we could of at least held hands that way. This was just too much, and I began to cry. The man next to me kept assuring me flying is the safest way to travel; he'd been flying for years. Finally, Boo told the stewardess we were just married and they got us together. As the 747 started to climb, the pressure pinned me against the seat. I turned to Boo and said, "Do I have to fly like this the whole six hours?" He laughed. I silently cried — it was so good to have him next to me.

Before our first anniversary we were blessed with a baby girl we named Mimi. There went our plans for planned parenthood. Everything was happening too fast in my life. I had only known Boo for eight months when we were married, and now I was a mother. I just didn't feel prepared. I don't even remember babysitting for any infants.

Her first night home from the hospital, I stayed awake all night waiting — and that was the only night our baby slept through the night, for the next nine months. After four nights of walking the floor with her, I called my mother who came over and put us to bed.

I was soon to find out that Mimi had colic and a hernia so I was not supposed to let her cry. I tried everything. I put a little sugar on her pacifier to help her fall asleep. One night I got lazy and put the sugar bowl in the end of her crib. Somehow during the night she put her wet little face in that bowl and in the morning our darling little girl was completely crystallized. A real sugar baby for sure!

I was trying to adjust to the loss of freedom. Boo needed our car to go to work, and I became very lonely. We had a small apartment, and I didn't have much to keep me busy even with a baby. My life seemed very empty, and I didn't feel that I was being fulfilled. I would wait all day for Boo to come home to talk to me. He was tired from working hard and all talked out from the guys on the job.

Deep within I began to feel maybe this was a mistake — that there just had to be more to life than this.

When Mimi was around seven months old, I went to the doctor so we could plan our next addition — only to find out I was pregnant again. What ever happened to our two-year interval between them? Consequently, by the time we were married two years, we had two children. We were blessed with a beautiful baby boy whom we named Matthew.

Most young women would have been thrilled. I just felt all the more trapped. It wasn't the fault of my babies or my husband. It was within me . . . married so soon after high school and now a family.

After my son was born, I began to overeat. From the time he was born in January until June of that year I gained sixty pounds. I can clearly remember one morning Mimi was in her high chair (she was about 16 months old) and with my right hand I was feeding her breakfast. Matthew, still a newborn, was cradled in my left arm as I fed him a bottle with my left hand; the phone rang.

There was no commercial from Calgonite to take me away. I felt cheated that I couldn't even talk on the phone. I know now it wasn't their fault, but I just felt like I was lost in all of this.

After Matt's first birthday, I kept after Boo to let me get a job. I thought that that would make me happy — to be out in the world of grown-ups again. He just didn't want me to work, so I kept eating and eating.

We didn't entertain or socialize. We were just kids trying to save our money to buy our first home. Boo became friends with a man at work who invited us to his New Year's Eve party. I went out shopping for just the right thing to wear, of course, and discovered that I needed a size 22½. I had really let myself go and was around 218.

At the party, in good fun I am sure, these people began to kid us about our sizes. They told Boo he must be henpecked to look at the size of his woman. I was crushed. I realized kids hurt and tease you, but I didn't think I would ever again feel that pain until that evening and this time it was from adults. I made the comment that if I could work, I wouldn't be fat. Boo said if I would lose 50 pounds, he would let me get a job.

Well, just call me Bugs; it was salads and lettuce for months, but I WAS DETERMINED, and I wanted to show those people at that party I could do it. After a few months and thirty pounds off, I saw the man whose house the party was in, at the store. He didn't even recognize me. When the rest of the weight was off — 65 pounds in all — I went and got a job. My children were three years and one and a half years old. Now, I've decided, I will become a career woman.

I set out to prove to Boo I could be Super Mom, Woman of the Year, and have a white glove inspection at my house any time. Well, I was busy all right, but still, inside was an emptiness I just couldn't handle. Why wasn't I happy? What more could I possibly need?

I worked for almost three years when Boo announced to me that he wanted me to stop working. He never wanted it, and he felt my place was in the home. I had a fear that while in this home I would once again end up in the kitchen and become fat and bored. I gave my two weeks notice with tears in my eyes because this kept me too busy to allow myself to feel the void I had inside.

As I left my job on the last day, I decided I would have no part of being home full time again. As I rode home, I made up my mind a divorce was the answer — then I could work if I wanted to and just live my life for me.

I packed all of my husband's possessions and put them on the front porch. I locked the front door and stood there in fear. When Boo arrived home to the surprise on our porch, his face became white. From behind the door he could hear me screaming that I wanted a divorce. He didn't even know we had marital problems!

There are times you can fool those around you, appearing very happy, when inside you are all eaten up. My husband and I began a separation that very night. Of course, as I look back, there was no reasoning with me. We had been married six years and never had a fight. I never spoke of anything I was unhappy about for fear of losing him. I always felt he was too good for me. Now I wanted to end it. I know this doesn't make much sense, but I was very confused at this time in my life and near to a nervous breakdown.

I wasn't sure I loved him, and then I was sure. We were off and on a couple of times. I was literally breaking his heart. Being afraid of what Boo might do in reaction to the way I was treating him, I made sure that I had a girlfriend stay with me each night.

This one evening I couldn't find anyone to stay with me. I almost went to the yellow pages in desperation. At age 26 now, I decided I better get my act together. Suddenly, in the middle of the night, I woke up to find Boo sitting on the side of the bed, telling me he loves me; that little bugger had broken in. As I went to get up, he held me by the shoulders and insisted that I talk to him. Over a pot of hot coffee, we talked well into the early morning hours.

The next morning from work I called a lawyer to discuss getting a restraining order to keep Boo away from the property. The lawyer couldn't figure out why I was so nervous as I sat in his office later, wringing my hands. He asked me if my husband cheated on me. "No, never!" was my reply. "Oh, well, he drinks?" he continued. "No, he doesn't drink." "He doesn't give you any money?" "Wrong again," I said. "He beats you?" he supposed. How could I tell this college graduate that it's because he doesn't put his wet towel in the hamper that I want a divorce.

As we discussed our separation and what had transpired during the evening before when Boo broke into the house, I found myself, almost before I knew it, at the police station signing a warrant for Boo's arrest for atrocious assault and battery. Now I really feared for my life!

I thought they would just call him up and tell him to leave me alone. I never dreamed they would send a car out to get him. I called his sister, Viki, and told her what I had done to her brother and how the police were looking for him. Later, I found out Boo went down to the police headquarters and turned himself in. He posted his bond and got released. I was sure this time he was out to get me.

I wasn't happy with him, and I wasn't happy without him. That Friday night I decided to go out with a girlfriend for a few drinks. At the bar that night a man asked me to dance. I don't want to lie or even exaggerate, but he looked just like Lurch — about seven feet tall.

It turned out that my Boo was there that night, too. I think he could handle my unhappiness and my confusion, but not this. I knew I had pushed him too far, and that I had lost him. Now I realized for certain that I really, really loved him with all my heart. It didn't matter if he was four feet tall and four feet wide. (He's not, you understand.)

He was my husband, flesh of my flesh, and I wanted him, but at this point, did he want me any longer?

CHAPTER III

A Lady Named Daniel?

God had not been a part of my life for over six years. In all that time never once did I even ask a blessing on the food.

During the time of separation from Boo, I became acquainted with a woman, Jackie, who kept telling me she was praying for us. I believe her prayers for us made the difference in our lives at this point in time.

Boo did come back once, but it lasted only a short time. Once again I had decided I wanted to be an independent career woman — on sixty-eight dollars a week?? When I told him to leave this particular time, Boo got down on his knees and asked the Lord not to allow this pain and hurt. He prayed for God to heal our marriage. My heart so hardened at this point, I placed my hands on my hips and laughed at him. I believe my words to him were, "Are you kidding? A grown man on his hands and knees and you think God's your answer — forget it!"

It's obvious that I had not turned to God or even thought of Him through all this troubled time. Jackie was faithful to pray, and God was faithful to answer.

The morning after the scene at the bar, I began to take a long look at my life. I just started crying. I didn't know what I wanted or why I was even here. At that moment the thought came to me that God was my answer. I didn't know where such a thought came from since I felt I had left my faith when I left my church. I have since found out there is such a difference between the two.

If God was my answer, I had to reach Him somehow. I spent the next half-hour trying to find my Rosary beads. Six years is such a long time. I looked everywhere. I just didn't think I could pray without them. Once found, I prepared to pray. I felt the only way God would hear me would be if I went to church.

A friend agreed to babysit with my children so I would be

21

free to go to church. It was about 7:00 p.m. and there was no evening Mass, so the church was empty when I got there. I was trying to pray the Rosary, but I couldn't feel the release I needed. I looked up at Jesus on the cross, remembering the many times as a child I would take down the crucifix above my bed and look at the suffering Savior. I would cry for His pain and I could never understand why He (God) would let them do that to Him.

This night, as I looked at Jesus, I was in pain. I cried out to Jesus to forgive me and to heal me. At that very instant all the lights went out in the church. There I was, alone with hundreds of flickering candles.

Amidst my cries and sobs I felt a man tapping me on the arm. He said I had to leave now so he could lock the church. Why didn't he go get me a priest . . . a nun . . . an altar boy? I really needed to talk to someone. By the time I got to my car, not only didn't my husband want me anymore, but now I felt God didn't want me. Being thrown out of God's house was more than I could bear.

I felt once again that no man loved or wanted me, and I purposed to take my life that night. I knew my mother would help Boo to raise our babies.

I thought about cutting my wrists, but I didn't think I could handle the blood. As a little girl I wanted so to be a nurse until my mother had her teeth pulled and I saw that blood — I passed out cold.

I considered driving into a pole, but knew I might end up, like my mother was in my childhood, paralyzed.

Pills seemed the only way to end it that night. Have you ever tried to overdose on Saint Joseph baby aspirin? There wasn't one other pill in our medicine cabinet. I couldn't even kill myself!

I just sat in the middle of the double bed with my legs crossed late into the night.

Jesus had to be real! How could I find Him? Touch Him? Feel Him? I had years and years of religion, but not a relationship with God.

Suddenly, from deep within, I prayed a prayer that was to change my life. I had never heard how to be saved or how to give your life to Christ. I did, however, somehow learn about

Daniel and how he had prayed three times a day.

From a very sincere heart I told God I would pray every day for the rest of my life three times a day if He would bring my husband home to me. I know it's faith that moves God, not deals, but I was doing all I knew to do at this time.

No, I wasn't born again at that moment, but God's Presence was upon me, and I knew without any doubt or reservation my marriage was healed and my husband was coming home. Now all I had to do was to tell Boo Boo.

I don't think I slept that night. I called Boo at 7:00 a.m. to come over right away. He sat down, never knowing what I would do next. I spoke out, "Boo Boo, God is healing our marriage. Come home." He looked at me like I was way out, got up, and left. I was not shaken. I knew he would be back. I didn't know how I knew, and I didn't care. I just knew he would be back, and I would pray three times a day.

Sure enough, Boo came back home that night, and I began to pray. I didn't have a Bible to read, and I didn't go to church. During this time Boo kept a very close watch on me. I don't blame him for not trusting me at this point.

Weeks turned into months and my friend, Jackie, did not limit her efforts to praying for us, but also came every Sunday morning to take our children to Sunday School. She knew how to reach the parents through their children.

After about six months Jackie invited me to her Methodist church to hear a Gospel Concert. Only once in my life had I been beyond the doors of a Protestant church. One Sunday I went for a walk near our home when I was growing up. The Baptist church around the block had its doors open. I had never heard such singing. In those days only the choir got to sing at Mass. I'd hear them sing, but I never saw them. It was as if the music floated down from heaven. But now, I decided to sit on their stoop and listen to this beautiful music. Soon a man was asking me to come in. When I told him I couldn't — I was a Catholic, he told me we are all God's children and I should come in and sing to God my Father.

There I was, hymnal in my hand and my toe tapping away, singing for the first time, "What a Friend We Have in Jesus." I remember the warm feeling I had all over, yet I was gripped with fear because I knew I was not supposed to be in there.

When the song ended, I ran home. I felt as though I had committed a sin and there was no grace left on my soul for the week to come. I could hardly wait for next Saturday night when I could go to confession and feel clean again. With that as my memory, I didn't respond to Jackie's invitation. Bless her heart, though, she persisted and every week she would invite me. Don't you ever give up on those you love and pray for!

As I thought it over, I realized I had stopped going to Mass, had missed Christmas, holydays of obligation, and Easter duty, and I knew I must be going to hell anyway, so what would it matter if I went to a Methodist church.

The very first thing I noticed was that the cross was empty. We covered Jesus during Lent, but we never took Him off. Since that time, however, I have been in a number of Catholic churches that have Jesus ascending in front of the crucifix. This time I just sat there stunned. Then, all the congregation started singing, "Let's Just Praise the Lord," with their hands raised in the air. Now I knew for sure why they told me not to come here! I thought they were crazy.

They had what is known as a Christian concert. I had never really heard anything like it before, but I enjoyed it. After the concert, the minister started to give the Gospel. He said Jesus loved me and died just for me. I always knew Jesus died for the world; I had been taught that as a child. I just didn't know where I fit into the world — it is so big. Did Jesus really die just for me?

He began to explain that if I would come to Jesus and ask Him into my heart, I would be saved. Saved from what? I just didn't understand. What was all this talk about — being born again and having the Holy Spirit come into you? Didn't the Trinity live in heaven together? I couldn't seem to understand all he was saying. He began to tell me how I could have my past forgiven and have a new beginning. I started to cry. I felt so guilty for all the sins I'd been carrying ever since I stopped going to church — six years of sin and guilt and, on top of that, the pain I had put my husband through.

An altar call was given, but I didn't go up because I didn't fully understand what was happening. To be born again at 27 — how?

I went home that night very confused, yet I wanted

everything the minister said I could have: forgiveness, love, acceptance, and a new beginning. I wanted Jesus in me, but I didn't know how to get Him there. The Scriptures tell us one job of the Holy Spirit is to bring to remembrance all that Jesus has said. That's what happened to me all that week; everything that was said kept running over in my mind. (Be encouraged: those you have witnessed to will be reminded.) I'd wake up in the morning wondering what it was to be saved; could I be?

The next Sunday Jackie called. I didn't want to go and yet I couldn't stay home. This time, after the music group sang and the invitation was given to receive Jesus as Lord and Savior, I went running down the aisle. I didn't care about anything or anyone there. I just wanted Jesus to be real to me.

A young singer from the group came and prayed with me. He told me I would be saved from hell — now I knew what I would be saved from. He said Jesus died for my sins and went to hell to pay for them for me. This was too easy and free; I didn't have to do anything except repent and believe on Jesus??

As I was leaving the church, the pastor stopped me and wanted to know if I received Jesus into my heart. "Oh, yes," I replied. He then asked me where I would go if I went outside and was hit by a car. Still smiling, if you can believe this, I told him I would go to hell. Poor man, the color just drained from his face. I told him I had to go home, and he said if I wanted to talk or if I needed him, just to call.

I didn't say anything to Boo when I got home that night. I didn't know if he ever heard about being saved. I thought the only people who were born again were those who belonged to this little Methodist church. I was soon to find out there are millions of born-again believers of all denominations.

I still had no assurance of heaven or my salvation or forgiveness when I awoke the next morning. But at work something was to happen that would change all that.

I was busy just working away when God spoke to me in an audible voice. I turned around when I heard the voice as real and as plain as could be, and there was no one there. I thought to myself: "Well, Gwen, you tried religion and now you are hearing voices — the men with the white jackets are going to come and take you away."

At that very moment I remembered the pastor the night before telling me to call him if he could help me. Right from work I called him to tell him that since I tried to get Jesus in my heart, I was now hearing voices. He asked me to come over to his study. I left work and drove right over.

It was then that he put the Word of God in my hand. I didn't really trust him because this was all so new to me. If it were true, why didn't someone tell me about this long ago? There was one thing I knew for sure — the Bible is God's Word. If this minister wasn't telling me the truth, or if the priest hadn't told me all about this, it didn't matter. The Bible was true, and I knew it. He then had me find Romans 10, and I started to read at verse 9.

"That if thou shalt confess with thy mouth the Lord Jesus, and shalt believe in thine heart that God hath raised him from the dead, thou shalt be saved. For with the heart man believeth unto righteousness; and with the mouth confession is made unto salvation. For the scripture saith, Whosoever believeth on Him shall not be ashamed . . . . . . For whosoever shall call upon the Name of the Lord shall be saved."

He asked me if I believed Jesus was God the Son Who died and rose for me. As I confessed Jesus with my mouth, and I did believe in my heart right then and there I was saved and born again. All my past sins were gone, and I knew it. I was made brand new. Nothing so wonderful had ever happened in all my life. For the first time in twenty-seven years I was no longer a fat slob and I knew that a man loved me. Jesus the Son of Man came into my heart by the Holy Spirit. I didn't need to be good enough. I was saved by the gift of God, not of works. It was a free gift that I had tried to work for as a young child for years. Now I knew what it was to know Jesus. I felt clean and white like never before. The Word of God is what caused me to believe. It didn't matter anymore what one church or another said. I wanted to know what God said.

In the third chapter of the Gospel of John, Jesus said, ". . . Except a man be born again, he cannot see the kingdom of God." And He said, "Marvel not that I said unto thee, Ye must be born again." (verses 3 and 7) — If you haven't been born again, marvel not. All you have to do is to confess your sins, turn from what you know to be wrong, and ask Jesus to come into your heart and be your personal Savior. Here's a prayer to help you if you want, but remember, God sees your heart; words are not the important thing:

"Father, I know I am a sinner. I believe that Jesus died and rose again from the dead for my sins and now by faith I receive You, Jesus, into my heart as my Savior. I repent of my sins, and I receive Your forgiveness and your love. Thank You, Jesus. In Your Name, I pray. Amen."

If you prayed that prayer, I welcome you into God's Family. Make sure you confess it with your mouth, won't you? Get yourself a Bible you can understand and begin to read it every day. Start in the Gospel of St. John.

I left that pastor's office a new person and under my arm was the New Testament in Modern Language which I began reading every chance I got.

I still didn't tell Boo, and he was still watching me. Every Sunday I went to church and never did invite him. As I look back now, I am now sure why I didn't.

I started playing Christian records, reading Christian testimony books — I couldn't get enough of the things of God.

One summer evening I was on the front porch with my nose buried in the Bible when Boo walked by and called me a Jesus freak under his breath. My kind and loving answer was, "Yea, well, the Bible says everyone has a cross to bear and you're my cross."

What I didn't realize was that I was making Jesus a threat to my husband. Jesus was and is first to me, but I didn't use any wisdom or judgment at all. I see this in many marriages now where only one person is saved. The Bible says the days are evil and we need to pray for God to redeem our time. If you will pray that, there will be ample time for Bible study, the tapes, records, etc., but there will also be time for your family. We need to keep a balance. We are trying to win them to the Lord, not drive them away. So many folks tell you if you want to come to Jesus, you have to stop smoking, dancing, listening to music, etc. True Christianity is not what you give up or even try to do without; it's what you receive — God's free gift of salvation through the Blood of Jesus Christ. God may indeed ask you to stop these other things, but to be saved, you only need to believe.

At this point I didn't know what Boo believed or didn't believe. I began to witness to everyone in my neighborhood and at work, never saying a word to Boo. One night I returned very late from witnessing to a friend and the Holy Spirit spoke to me to wake Boo up and ask him to receive the Lord Jesus. "Oh sure," I thought, "I'll just tap him on the shoulder in the middle of the night and ask him to be born again. No way!"

I couldn't sleep all that night; I felt like Jacob when he wrestled that angel. By morning I was so tired; Boo came along all rested and full of life. I was cooking pancakes at the time and without the love of God I turned on him like a crazy lady, shaking the pancake flipper at him, yelling, "Do you want to accept Jesus into your heart and be saved?"

To my utter amazement my Boo said, "Yes." I cried. He cried. We just wept together as my husband came back to the Lord. I found out later that Boo had made a commitment to the Lord as a young man but had fallen away. Now he was coming home to stay. God's timing is perfect.

The greatest witness I gave Boo was the witness of my life. I was a changed life — a new woman right before his eyes. I was happy and content for the very first time in my life.

Don't worry if your mate isn't saved. Allow your light to shine before them. Sometime after this I found a Scripture I had never seen before. It was as if the Lord put it in the Bible just for me that day. "Likewise, ye wives, be in subjection to your own husbands; that, if any obey not the word, they also may without the word be won by the conversation of the wives" (I Peter 3:1).

What a promise for you today — that they will be won over without the word — by your conversation or behavior. As they see more and more of Jesus in you, their conversation gets closer and closer. Trust God! Take Him at His Word, won't you?

We were now this happy family. Boo started to go to church with us. I was just thrilled with the Word of God. Having never read a Bible, I was so excited. I wanted to learn all about Jesus — everything He said or did. I still do — I pray I never lose my hunger for the Word of God.

I bought a small New Testament that I could carry to work to read at lunch and during breaks. I was working in Atlantic

City and used to park at a particular lot. I didn't know the attendant. I would leave a check on his desk at the beginning of each month. Our 1971 Chevy was now showing signs of age, so we decided to get the whole car repainted. The paint was hardly dry this one day. I was so careful where I parked — I didn't want anyone's door to hit our beautiful car.

I no sooner got busy at work when a friend told me the man from the parking lot wanted to see me. He didn't have any idea what floor I worked on or what department I worked in; he had gone from counter to counter, looking for the blond who drove a green '71 Chevy. When I saw him , my heart sank. My new paint job — I just knew my car had been hit. In the three years I had worked and parked in his lot, he never came to my place of employment.

As soon as I saw him, I wanted to know how bad it was. He would not tell me. Even in the elevator he just asked me to wait until we got outside. I knew now my '71 four-door Chevy was going to look like a Volkswagen. Right then I told God I was sorry I was so worldly, and I asked Him to help me be calm when I saw my very first "new" car all mangled.

Once outside this man asked me if I was a born-again Christian. I told him I was and asked why he wanted to know and how did he know. He told me the Lord told him I was saved and to go get me.

His lot was next door to the unemployment office. A man had come out to get into his car and as he went to pay, he made a remark about his checks being stopped and wanting to end it all. My friend, Mr. Parking Lot, (I never did find out his name) began to witness to this troubled man about Jesus and during this time the Holy Spirit told him to get me. He asked me to share my testimony of Jesus with this man. "Amen," I said, "let's go." When we got to the parking lot, the man had waited. There I was with the New Testament in my purse. I shared the Love of God with him and as he cried ever so softly, we prayed with him the sinner's prayer.

When I got back to work I had been gone forty-five minutes. Of course, everyone wanted to know how the car was and if I had to have it towed, etc. It was at this moment I realized I had been part of a miracle.

The way God is changing me is a miracle in itself. I had

always been conservative with money — cheap is what I was. I remember once my brother, Dirk, asked my mother and me to go to the race track with him. I had only been married a short time, and we really didn't have money for such an adventure. It was Lady's Day so we got in for free. We went in Dirk's car, so I didn't even have to pay for parking. So far, I was having fun.

My mother and I each put in a dollar for a two-dollar bet on the first race. Our horse lost, and I was through with that place. For the next six races all I did was complain about losing my money and what a rip-off it was. At the end of the day my brother took me aside with such a worried look on his face. He put a fifty dollar bill in my hand and told me not to worry — Boo wouldn't have to find out how much I lost. He figured I had lost our grocery money and wanted to be sure we would be okay for the coming week.

It was then I had the nerve to tell him I lost only a dollar. As I tried to give him back his money, he went bananas. Every time I think of that day, I laugh.

Not long after that, I started reading in the Word of God about how God loves a cheerful giver. I was trying to allow Him to be Lord of my finances, and I was giving. At first I gave just out of obedience — forget the cheerfulness. One thing at a time.

Soon I realized I was feeling joy in giving, and I was no longer cheap. Even to this day, however, I try to be a good steward of God's money.

On Labor Day Dirk and his family came over to our house. Before the telethon went off the air, I wanted to make a pledge. We were sitting outside at the picnic table, and I asked Boo to come in for a moment — I wanted to see him. His reply was that we were all family — what did I want. I knew the Scripture saying not to let your right hand know what your left hand is doing, so I didn't want to make any big announcements. I did want Boo's approval on the amount I wanted to pledge.

Finally, I was in a position where I had to tell him. I asked him if it was all right to call in fifty dollars. Well, my brother fell off the picnic table, yelling, "Not Gwen; not my sister — fifty dollars?" Lying on the ground he shouted, "She's so

30

cheap, she squeaks." We were all laughing by then, but as I headed for the house to make the call, Dirk followed, wanting to hear me make the call with his own ears.

After I called, he asked me what had changed me. What an opportunity to tell him of my Jesus. I realized that day that God can move even when it is something that has nothing to do with "religion." Had our pledge been to a church, I don't think Dirk would have noticed. Give the Lord all the areas of your life, and He will use them.

I just want to share one more thing that to me is a miracle. It is how the Word of God delivered me from fear and has kept me free from it.

Never have I enjoyed going to the dentist. My first experience of a dentist as a child was one who would drill a hole in a perfectly good tooth while I was numb so that very soon I would be back with another cavity.

Once married, I decided no more of that for me. I'd just wait until they had to be pulled, go to sleep, and have the teeth taken out. My children went every six months for check-ups and at one of these times a very nice dentist, Dr. Clark, asked me when was my last check-up. He seemed kind, and so I did go twice over the next ten years. I was so frightened — I'd rather suffer.

I was there with my daughter one day when he once again talked me into coming in myself. The receptionist made a comment that it had been over three years since I had been there. I realized that the last time I wasn't yet a Christian. Instead of praying, I thought this would just be a piece of cake because I now have Jesus.

As the dental assistant began to clean my teeth, I started to cry. Such great fear came over my shaking body, I almost became paralyzed. I don't remember ever being that afraid before. The assistant really had a hard time. She kept telling me how sorry she was, asking if I was all right and if she was hurting me. Finally, that ordeal was over. She took me into the other room where I was to wait for Dr. Clark.

In walks some dentist I never saw before. All I kept saying was that I wanted Dr. Clark. This man realized he would not be able to get me to sit down, let alone check my teeth. He told me to make another appointment when Dr. Clark could see me. I was humiliated but I did make a new appointment.

I left there very angry and upset with myself and with God. I'd been hearing sermons about all this power I have now that God's Spirit lives in me. Where was that power? If it was there, how do I use it?

At home I began to look into what the Word of God had to say concerning fear. Hebrews 13:5-6 just jumped off the page: ". . . I will never leave thee, nor forsake thee. So that we may boldly say, The Lord is my helper, and I will not fear what man shall do unto me."

Because this verse said, "we . . . say," I decided to start speaking the Word of God to my fear and to myself and to Satan. For over a week I kept repeating this verse, knowing that the dentist was only a man. What could he do to me?

The morning finally arrived for me to put the Word of God to the test. I tell you honestly that I would ask for my mouth to be numb even when my teeth were cleaned. I arrived on time, but was told my appointment was not for another hour. I wondered, "Is this some kind of test from the Lord?" "Would He really want me to sit listening to the drill for an hour?"

I decided to spend the time at the Christian book store close by. Right off the shelf a book started calling me . . . "Tortured for Christ." That just matched my mood. I bought it and began reading it while waiting for my turn to come.

Some of the people had really suffered for the Lord. One lady was hung upside down and her teeth were kicked out. No sooner had I read about it, the door opened and I was called in.

As I walked into that clean, modern office, I felt ashamed of how afraid I'd been. I began to thank and praise God for the clean and up-to-date equipment and for the dentist who was only a man and could do nothing to me since Jesus would never leave me. As he began to check my teeth, I kept repeating in my head words of praise and thanks to Jesus.

He told me I had a cavity, and then he asked me if I would like some Novocaine. I told him, "No." After that came out of my mouth, I just sat there stunned. What had I done? As he began to drill my tooth, I quoted the Word of God to myself. I knew God's Word is true and I had no fear in me. I was so calm, I almost fell asleep. As I looked at that dentist, I thought, "Jesus won't ever leave me, and you are just a man.

I'll not fear what you can do unto me ever again."

For months, every time I brushed my teeth, I couldn't keep from smiling. Could you?

CHAPTER IV

Tongues of Fire? Too Hot For Me!

Now that Boo had rededicated his life to Jesus, he started going with me to the Methodist church where I received the Lord. For those next few months everything was grand. I read my Bible daily, went to church twice on Sunday; I was really becoming a fanatic!

I became involved in fellowship with the women from my church. One summer evening I was at the home of a friend, Barbara. We were becoming close friends until that evening when Barbara mentioned a second experience in her Christian walk after the new birth — the Baptism in the Holy Spirit.

I thought it was just great until she told me she prayed in tongues. "You do what?" I could feel the color leaving my face and the palms of my hands becoming cold and clammy. It was now time to go home, and I didn't know if I would ever return.

I never heard of such a thing as praying in tongues. It sounded too strange a thing for me to understand, and I didn't like that word, "tongues." However, I had such a deep desire for more of God. I wanted, or so I thought, all God had to offer. A few nights later I prayed for tongues, only because Barbara had them. It didn't matter to me that she was saved three years and I was just a baby in Christ. I figured if I did this, I would be just like her tomorrow — very mature and very spiritual overnight.

When I prayed, nothing happened. My prayer went like this, "Father, I'll take tongues so I can be spiritual like Barbara, in Jesus' Name. Amen." Do you wonder why God didn't answer?

James 4:2-3 (NIV) says: ". . . You do not have, because you do not ask God. When you ask, you do not receive, because you ask with wrong motives, that you may spend what you get on your pleasures."

The only reason I asked was to be like Barbara. The Father wants us to be like Jesus, not another Christian. This is a lesson I have learned over and over. Be careful you don't get your eyes on other believers; keep your eyes on Jesus, the

Author and Finisher of your faith. (Hebrews 12:2).

I thought no more about this tongues business. God didn't answer, so I assumed I was not to have them. I resumed my life, but wasn't too crazy about going over to Barbara's house. As a matter of fact, I thought Barbara was crazy. Has anyone thought that about you?

A few weeks went by and our minister invited a Pentecostal minister to preach the Word at our Wednesday night service. I still didn't have any idea what it was to be a Pentecostal, even though Boo grew up one. He now went to church with me, and we never did discuss this. (Good thing!)

My Methodist church was a quiet group of believers. On this particular night our guest preacher was really giving us the Word of God. I was soaking it up. The service to this point was a blessing to me. Towards the end of the service he asked those desiring prayer to form a line at the side of the church. He was going to lay hands on the people. Do what?

I was in an attitude of prayer — little tears just dropping quietly off my cheeks, when the first lady he prays for drops to the floor. They call it 'slain in the Spirit.' I call it unconscious! The woman was out cold. Poor thing, did she faint or have a heart attack? No one seemed to care. There she is on the floor, people walking all around her saying, "Oh, bless God."

The tears just stopped in mid-stream right there on my face. You can bless God if you want to; I am going home. This is just too much for me.

I reached for my Bible, wondering how I could leave without causing a disturbance. The next fellow the preacher lays hands on starts shouting, "Oh, thank You, Jesus." When he began to shake as well, I was gone! I ran out the back of that church, and I think if anyone had tried to stop me, in love, I would have beat them to death with my purse.

I was so scared, I was shaking. As I was running — and I mean running — home, I kept thinking maybe it's time for me to go back to the Catholic Church. I figured I could find a church with the mass still in Latin — no more worries about this kind of thing and when I die, I'll go to heaven. (I didn't know anything about the Charismatic Renewal in the Catholic Church — how God was pouring out His Spirit on all flesh.) All I knew was I wanted to get home where I could feel safe and secure. I came tearing in the front door and began telling Boo how awful it was over there at our church — how they were falling on the floor, shouting and shaking — it was terrible. He told me to get his slacks, he was going over there. (Oh my, had I married one of them???)

The next two weeks were just terrible for me. I wouldn't pray because I just knew as soon as I said grace, my eyes were going to roll around in my head, and God was going to make me a Pentecostal. I knew I'd probably start shaking and then this Spirit would take me over and I'd speak in tongues and then it would stop and I would be sane again. (Up until this time I had never heard a message in tongues with interpretation — I don't think I could have handled it.)

About three weeks after this experience in church, I decided to call my pastor and tell him what a terrible service that was, a grown woman lying on the floor, men hollering — honestly, did he know he would have to account to God for that carrying on? Pastor then told me that the minister that night had wanted the young man to receive the gift of tongues. (Oh, no, don't tell me my pastor knew about tongues, too!) During the phone conversation my pastor realized how upset and frightened I really was and he asked me to come see him.

My husband was working, so I took Mimi and Matthew to a sitter. I entered the pastor's study full of fear and yet I didn't know why I was so terrified.

He began to try to counsel me, explaining how he felt God wanted to give me the gift of tongues. I told him to tell God I didn't want that gift. Since I hadn't prayed in almost three weeks, God and I were not on speaking terms.

My pastor really had a hard time understanding me. He wanted to know if I ever heard anyone pray in tongues. I said, "No!" Then he told me he did. (Oh, help! Please help!!)

There I sat — a twenty-nine year old adult who at that very minute stuck my fingers in my ears and started saying, "Don't you do it . . . I'll never come here again." I could see his lips move just a little and with that, I said, "If it's not English, I'll scream!" By now I had moved all the way down the couch so I could be close to the door. I took my fingers out of my ears.

Pastor just looked at me and told me he couldn't help me. I was afraid to trust God and give my whole self to the Lord —

that I was afraid of the power of the Holy Spirit. He was right — I sure was afraid and now disappointed that he couldn't help me. (As I look back, I am so glad he said all that to me because I had a dependency on people and not on God.)

Well, I went home and decided to trust God. I knew I was going to have an "upper room," so I locked all the doors. I even left a note — "To Whom It May Concern." I knew I was going to become Pentecostal. I figured I might shake and scream — who knows?

I read again Acts 2:1-4, "And when the day of Pentecost was fully come, they were all with one accord in one place. And suddenly there came a sound from heaven as of a rushing mighty wind, and it filled all the house where they were sitting. And there appeared unto them cloven tongues like as of fire, and it sat upon each of them. And they were all filled with the Holy Ghost, and began to speak with other tongues, as the Spirit gave them utterance."

As I walked upstairs to have my "upper room," my heart was pounding. I sat on the side of my bed, and I watched the curtains. I knew very soon they would start to blow (that mighty rushing wind, you know.)

I prayed a very simple prayer, but I prayed it in faith. I asked Jesus to fill me with the Holy Spirit even if I had to speak in tongues. The Holy Spirit descended on me in a way I'll never forget.

I was afraid of the baptism of the Holy Spirit and fire. God sent me a dove. I was so afraid of being burned. The Spirit of God in love and great gentleness filled me that afternoon as I sat there.

I had the sensation of warm oil being poured all over me. Then in my mind I heard two little words that were not English. What was this? They seemed to be all I could think so I decided to say them. After I said them, I got a few more little syllables and as I spoke them, I was now praying in tongues. It was marvelous. Every time I would say these strange words, I would get the chills. I never did scream or shake, but I was immersed in the fullness of the Holy Spirit. It was a Baptism of Love!

I felt great. I was amazed that I could start to pray in tongues and stop any time I wanted to. I never had any teaching on the subject, so I knew nothing. I sat there, for I don't know how long; then, I jumped up and ran over to the mirror to see if you could tell I was now one of them. Oh, boy, was I!

My husband was working on the night shift, so I stayed up all night praying in tongues. The next day the first thing I did was to run to the Christian book store. Under my right arm I got every book I could carry that had anything to do with the Baptism in the Holy Spirit. Under my left arm I had all the books that had anything to do with praying in tongues.

I know now the book I really should have read and studied was the Bible. Everything we need for life and godliness is in the scriptures. Everything I needed to know about the Baptism and tongues is also in the Word of God.

At this time I didn't realize Satan didn't want me to use this gift God had given me. I started reading all these different books.

I am amazed at how I had such a real touch from God and now only a few days later I would doubt.

In one of the books I read about a Pentecostal minister who said he prayed in tongues and was now sure he made it up in his flesh. He said that once he renounced it, God's blessing was upon his life.

That was it. I was sure I was making this language up. I prayed a prayer of repentance. I started telling God I was sorry I made these words up and that if He would forgive me, I would never use it again. I went to bed that night sure that God was pleased with me, while in reality, only the enemy thought he had won.

The next morning, as I was preparing breakfast, my little girl, Mimi, was sitting at the kitchen table coloring in her coloring book. She looked so cute and sweet sitting there. She was only five years old now and her little pigtails would shake as she was coloring away. Without any warning, she started praying out loud in my prayer tongues. No one had ever heard me, and I received such a witness inside that this was of God. I started crying, and I knew that this gift was real, of God, and for today. I told God (in between the sobs) that I would use it always, and I was so thankful He showed me the truth.

At this point someone may ask, "How did you know it

wasn't from Satan?" First of all, my little girl had already ask-ed Jesus into her heart. Didn't Jesus rebuke the disciples when they tried to keep the little children away?

The main reason I know what I received wasn't from the devil is because I asked in Jesus' Name. I didn't go somewhere looking for a spirit. I asked to be filled with God the Holy Spirit in the Name of Jesus. John 14:14 gives us the Words of Jesus: "If ye shall ask any thing in My Name, I will do it."

You see, in all four gospels we are told Jesus would baptize in the Holy Spirit. I asked Jesus, and 'f we can ask in His Holy Name and Satan can give it to us, we are without hope.

Some have brought I Corinthians 13:8-10 to my attention, saying that tongues stopped with the apostles. Reading from the NIV, "Love never fails. But where there are prophecies, they will cease; where there are tongues, they will be stilled; where there is knowledge, it will pass away. For we know in part and we prophesy in part, but when perfection comes, the imperfect disappears."

When Jesus comes, Who is Perfection, it's true that all these will disappear. I won't need to pray in tongues when Jesus comes. The Bible tells you that he who speaks in tongues speaks unto God and not unto men. When I pray in the spirit, I am speaking to God. It also says (I Corinthians 13:12), "For now we see through a glass, darkly; but then face to face: now I know in part; but then shall I know even as also I am known." When I am with God, I won't need to speak to Him in tongues.

After the Holy Spirit spoke through my daughter, I realized tongues must be very useful or very powerful for Satan to try to keep me from using the gift. I started to study what the Word of God has to say about praying in tongues.

First, I saw that you're speaking unto God and it is also for your edification: (I Corinthians 14:4), "He that speaketh in an unknown tongue edifieth himself . . ."

It is also a form of thanksgiving and praise (I Corinthians 14:16 NIV), "If you are praising God with your spirit, how can one who finds himself among those who do not understand say 'Amen' to your thanksgiving, since he does not know what you are saying?"

There are times when I am full of thanksgiving towards all that the Lord is doing for me. I can only say, "Thank You,

Jesus," a number of times until I feel as though I'm not expressing all that I feel. That's one of the times you can go into tongues for praise and thanksgiving. The great thing is that you don't need your understanding.

I remember one experience in prayer while on my knees in fellowship with God, the thought crossed my mind, "Did I get something out of the freezer for dinner?" I felt really bad about that.

Tongues is a way to praise and worship without your mind. I never learned this language. When I use it, I am edified because it daily is a miracle to me.

The Bible says to pray without ceasing. I have found this one way to fulfill that Scripture. When I am driving the car and I am alone, I can intercede and pray in the Holy Spirit.

May I say at this point to those of you who have not yet received this gift, it is available to any born-again believer.

Jesus, in Acts 1:4-5 told those assembled to wait for the promise of the Father. He told them that John did baptize with water, but they would soon be baptized with the Holy Spirit. That is what did happen in Acts, chapter 2, when they were all filled with the Spirit and began to speak in tongues.

In Acts 19 we find Paul dealing with disciples who had never even heard of the Holy Spirit. Paul pursued this further, asking them what baptism they had received. They told him: ". . . John's baptism." In verse six, Paul laid hands on them and they received the Holy Spirit, speaking in tongues and prophesying. These were believers already, yet Paul clearly asked them about the baptism they had received.

In Acts 10:44-48, the Holy Spirit fell on all the Gentiles there who heard the Word while Peter was yet speaking. They spoke with tongues and magnified God — the evidence to Peter that these indeed were now believers and should be baptized with water.

The very first person the Lord ever directed me to lay hands on for the baptism of the Holy Spirit was a woman named Nellie, who He told me he was seeking this gift. I didn't feel I could do this, so I just avoided Nellie. I would sit on the opposite side of the church. When she came in, I would go out. One Sunday evening, however, Nellie came over to me. She said her car was not running. She had gotten a ride to church and was wondering if I could take her home.

The presence of the Holy Spirit was evident on the drive home, and I didn't want to be disobedienct. Right there and then, I pulled off the road and asked Nellie if she was seeking the Holy Spirit and the gift of tongues. Of course, her answer was yes, but was I ready for this? I had never ever prayed out loud in tongues, yet here I was in the woods with sweaty palms and Nellie looking at me like, "What's next?"

I laid hands on her, prayed for her to be filled, and softly I prayed in the Spirit. Nothing else, folks! I didn't give her any instructions. I just took her home and had her get out of my car (Fast).

On my way home I was really upset. "Hadn't God told me to lay hands on her? Didn't I pray right? Why didn't she speak in tongues as the Spirit gives utterance?" All of a sudden I knew I needed to believe. All this doubt and unbelief wasn't pleasing to God.

I began to thank Jesus for filling her. I thanked Him that I am in the Spirit — not in the flesh, since the Spirit of Jesus lives in me. I walked in my front door and the phone was ringing. I picked up the receiver to hear Nellie crying and speaking in tongues.

I have since had many opportunities to help people receive the gift of the Holy Spirit. It was a few years after I was filled with the Spirit that God did something for my husband.

Even though he knew I prayed in tongues and even though he had a Pentecostal background, he didn't seem to want this gift. I think his attitude was, if Jesus wants to baptize me in the Holy Spirit, He will do it. God wants all to be saved, and yet there comes a time you need to turn to God and receive. It is the same with the gift of the Holy Spirit.

Luke 11:11-13 says, "If a son shall ask bread of any of you that is a father, will he give him a stone? Or if he ask a fish, will he for a fish give him a serpent? Or if he shall ask an egg, will he offer him a scorpion? If ye then, being evil, know how to give good gifts unto your children: how much more shall your heavenly Father give the Holy Spirit to them that *ask* Him?"

I left tracts everywhere he sat. Didn't do a thing. He didn't even read them. About four years after I was filled, we went to hear a lady speaker at a local high school auditorium. She never even preached on it, but at the end of her service she said, "If you want the Baptism in the Holy Spirit, come up front." There, in a crowd of hundreds, up gets my Boo Boo. Not a word to me and down to the front he goes. "Didn't he know I knew how to pray? Would God really fill him without me?"

There were so many who went forward, they took them in the back. A short time later someone asked me to go in the back and help them minister.

Total confusion reigned. No one seemed to be in charge or even to know what was happening or what they were doing. Looking for Boo, I saw some man banging Boo's head against the wall and shouting in tongues in his ear. (Oh, dear Lord, a total turnoff, I am sure.) A few of us who knew the Word eventually got things calmed down and we instructed a small circle of folks who, when allowed to believe the Word of God, received with no problem. I didn't know where Boo was during this time.

Afterwards, we went to the local diner with another couple. I felt uneasy and was worried about my husband. I asked him if anything happened to him. (I didn't mean a concussion, either!") Even in all that, he received a few syllables.

At home that night, after we had gone to bed, I awoke and Boo was not beside me. I just started praying for him. In the morning he shared with me that he just didn't know if all that happened at that school was of God — and for him. He began to read his Bible. No sooner had he prayed and asked God to show him the truth, his Open Bible study helps he was preparing to read, fell open to: "But Pentecost with the Spirit's mighty filling, had brought a radical change."

My husband on his knees began to weep and pray in tongues for almost an hour. The Holy Spirit touched him in a real way.

Those people who ministered to him earlier meant well, I am sure. If you have ever had someone try to minister this to you and maybe you didn't receive, go to the Lord yourself.

Many people think they need to get their life all cleaned up before the Holy Spirit will fill them. This is just not so. I was still addicted to cigarettes when I received the gift of the Holy Spirit. I had one woman tell me I'd never receive this gift if I smoked because God wouldn't fill a dirty vessel. I just didn't have the heart to tell her I was already Spirit-filled.

What we need is child-like faith. Just recently I was in the kitchen listening to a tape when Matthew came in from playing. He's now twelve; only once did he ever hear anything about tongues. I had taken my children with me one Sunday evening to an Assembly of God church where the gifts of the Spirit were in open operation. We still belong to a church where they are not, but we know that is where we belong and the Lord is blessing all there.

At this service, however, a lady right behind my children gave a message in tongues. All the way home I tried to explain it to them. Days later they were still asking about it.

One night at dinner they decided to ask their Daddy about this. Boo explained it the best he could. He was telling them that many Christians pray in tongues. "Do they, Daddy?" "Do they?" Boo went on to tell them his grandmother prayed in tongues. "Did she, Daddy?" "Did she?" Then Boo says, (as I'm eating my dinner, very nonchalant), "My wife prays in tongues." "Does she, Daddy?" "Does she?" All of a sudden it hit them that his wife was their mother. In unison they both turned and looked at me and asked, "Do you, Mommy?" "Do you?"

As I was listening to this tape this time, on came a message in tongues. Matt wanted to hear it again. I rewound it and played it for him. I then explained how Jesus would fill him with His Spirit if Matt would ask and that he would then receive a language of his own to pray in. I asked him if he wanted me to pray with him. "No," was his reply and out he went to play.

The subject came up somehow only a few days later. Matt wanted to know if anyone he knew prayed in tongues. I named just a few that were close family members and told him, "Your Dad and I do," and little Matt said he did, too. I said, "What?" He then told me how, after I told him to ask the Lord that night, he asked and Jesus did give him his own prayer language, baptizing him in the Holy Spirit.

You see: he believed. He never heard that it's not for today or that it's of the devil. He believed my word. Won't you believe Jesus' Words? As Peter went to preach the words of salvation in Acts 10, he retells the event in Acts 11:15-16:

"And as I began to speak, the Holy Ghost fell on them, as on us at the beginning. Then remembered I the word of the Lord, how that He said, John indeed baptized with water; but ye shall be baptized with the Holy Ghost."

You need tarry no longer. Read Luke 11:11-13. Pray the prayer of faith and receive. Just ask Jesus to baptize you with the Holy Spirit. In faith, receive the gift of tongues. I have seen God fill hundreds of people with the Holy Spirit. Don't speak in English (or your own tongue) anymore. You can't speak in two languages at the same time. As you hear words in your mind or sense them in your spirit, just speak them out. Remember: It's praise and thanksgiving!

A short time after my Baptism in the Holy Spirit, I sensed that it was now time to quit my job. I was afraid that I would just stay home and get fat again. I also had the fear that the past would repeat itself. I had no guarantees. I told no one at all how I felt deep inside. The nudging continued and finally I gave my notice. I didn't cry this time, but I wasn't happy either.

I left the job on a Friday with all these hidden fears. The next morning I had been invited to my very first Full Gospel Businessmen's meeting in a hotel over in Atlantic City.

There was a huge crowd, and it was my first time in charismatic worship. After breakfast the guest speaker from Texas was introduced.

Before he began to speak he said God wanted him to minister to a young lady in green and white. I started looking around when all of a sudden I noticed my blazer was green and white. (Oh, no, was that really my arm?) I pointed to myself, and he nodded I was the one.

He prophesied over me the following: "I know you have just made a change in your life, and you are fearful. Fear not. The past will never repeat itself. You are to stay at home in the Word of God. God is going to use you in a mighty way."

I never knew God could speak through someone like that. I knew it was God for sure, because I had told no one. I never saw that brother from Texas again. I doubt if I saw him now I would even know him, but I am thankful for his openness to the Spirit of God.

CHAPTER V

Women's Aglow and Lady Buxton

I never did give that prophecy much thought, especially the part about God using me in a mighty way. I did, however, stay at home with the Word of God.

At times I wondered what I would do with all my free time. I just told God I was available for anything He wanted me to do.

I was acquainted with a lady named Terri from my church. I did not know her real well, but I had been to a prayer meeting at her house once.

This Wednesday I was on my way food shopping. I thought to myself that I must get to see Terri. I didn't follow through with that thought at the time. I finished my entire food order and on the way home, it was almost as if my car just wouldn't go another way. I had to go to Terri's. I parked the car and ran to her door. Her Mom informed me Terri wasn't home. How's that for being Spirit-led?

I hadn't even put all the food away when Terri called, so excited. God had answered her fleece.

Terri received a letter in the mail informing her that some women in Ocean City were going to start a Women's Aglow Fellowship. They asked her to pray about becoming involved and to bring with her anyone she felt God wanted to be a part of this ministry. When Terri read that letter, my name dropped into her spirit — or was it her mind?

Terri asked the Lord to confirm this. If He wanted me to go with her to this meeting, I would come by her house. You can see why she was so thrilled — I had never just stopped by her house before. (I believe there are two reasons why she wasn't home. One — I obeyed, but delayed until I was done shopping. Two — When we start having fellowship, time flies and my food could have spoiled.)

I was really impressed at the way God answered her fleece. I decided to go with her to this planned meeting.

I had never heard of Women's Aglow, and I had no idea who

they were or what they did. I soon found out they were charismatic women who held a luncheon or breakfast, etc. once a month with a guest speaker . . . very similar to the Full Gospel Businessmen, only it's a ministry of women to women.

The only jobs I'd ever held were in offices doing bookkeeping and handling money — making deposits and balancing journals.

As I sat there thinking all this over, the woman who God called to be the President shook her pen right at me and said, "I am sure God sent someone here to be our treasurer." (That's me! That's me!)

Terri never did feel God calling her to serve, but she knew I was to be a part of this fellowship. We began to meet once a week for prayer. We continued to meet every week for months before we ever had our first outreach meeting.

Here I was in a room full of women I didn't know and yet, as we began to meet for prayer together, there was such a bond of love between us. Jesus said the world will know we are His disciples by our love.

I found love and fellowship with these women who soon became like sisters to me. In order for us to really get to know one another, they decided that once a month one of us would give our testimony to just this little group of ladies. This would give us a better understanding of each other — why maybe we react the way we do, etc. Finally, it was my turn.

I had never told anyone all that is now in this book, but as I shared my life, one minute they were laughing, the next they were crying. They all felt I had been gifted of God to speak. (Who, me?) I was nervous in front of these eight or nine women. Every month at our Aglow outreach meeting, as treasurer, I would have to take an offering. I was so nervous, I would be sick before each meeting. I would have cramps and be in a cold sweat by the time it was time to take the offering. How could I ever get up in front of a group?

I wouldn't talk at a Tupperware party even, let alone in front of a crowd. Even though I was growing in the Lord and really did feel secure, there was still something not right.

One of these ladies who I love dearly said she felt I had a spirit of rejection. Now let's not get into spirits. The only spirit I was interested in was the Holy Spirit. I saw too many Christians finding demons under every rock, and yet what she said stayed on my mind.

We then heard another Women's Aglow chapter was having a speaker who had a ministry of "You got it" deliverance. A number of us decided to go and hear her. Well, the Lord knew just the kind of woman I needed to see that day. First off, she was in her sixties, cute, quiet, little thing with grey hair. I felt safe enough. She gave us a good teaching from the Word of God that afternoon, and it was now time to go. I thought I'd stop to say goodbye and let her know I enjoyed her talk. Next thing I know I hear someone crying and sobbing real deep. I thought, "Poor thing." Here, it's me. Somehow, there I was with my head in her chest, both hands over my face. As I went to sit up, tears shot out of my hands like rockets over the pew in front of us. She then said that the Lord had set me free from a spirit of self-rejection. I am not going to attempt to explain this. Was it a demon? A spirit? In me? On me? Around me? All I know is that after that, I was different. I could be in front of people and feel confident in Jesus. (I am reminded at this point of the blind man in the ninth chapter of the Gospel of John. In response to the questions of the Pharisees, he answered them in verse 25: "Whether he be a sinner or no, I know not: one thing I know, that, whereas I was blind, now I see.")

During and after all those young years of fat, I really felt I had nothing of value to say. I would reject myself before anyone else could; that way, I was safe from being hurt. "Where the Spirit of the Lord is, there is liberty."

By this time my mother and father had started to come to church with me. That was not that easy. Because she went to church, my Mom felt she was a Christian. I was witnessing to her every chance I got. The people who are good are often the hardest to reach.

I finally asked her if the Spirit of Jesus was in her. The Bible says in Romans 8:9, ". . . Now if any man have not the Spirit of Christ, he is none of His." I loved her and my Daddy, and I wanted them to be saved. One Sunday night at church our pastor said the altar was open for prayer if anyone wanted to pray for their loved ones.

I went and knelt and prayed that night for my parents to give their lives over to Jesus. In a few moments' time, someone tapped me on the shoulder and said my mother needed me. Well, I got up and turned around to head back to our pew. I bumped into my father coming down the aisle to the altar where my mother was crying. They both gave their hearts to the Lord, and at their age, it was hard to admit they needed Him. Praise the Lord, they did!

Long about this time, I was feeling bad because I was still smoking. Even at the Aglow luncheons, I would crave a cigarette so bad, I would end up in the Ladies' Room (hiding in there, if you know what I mean) blowing smoke into the water. At my age, really? I just couldn't stop. I prayed. I cried. I tried to bargain with God. Nothing helped.

I started going to different people for prayer, just looking for the one with the touch, and I would be delivered. I had one lady tell me she was so glad I wasn't going to hell because I smelled like I had been there. That really hurt me and I cried and cried. Why couldn't I do this for Jesus? He died for me. Then, I just got plain mad that this had such a hold over me. I was smoking two and a half packs a day, and on top of that, I was addicted to a strong menthol brand.

I had tried to stop once before when I was still working; I thought it would be a good witness for those with whom I worked. I had stopped for almost three weeks, and I went around telling all my non-Christian employees that Jesus had delivered me from smoking. At the end of the three weeks, I had gained seventeen pounds. I was miserable. The withdrawal was terrible, and I was mad at God that He wanted me to quit.

I started to sneak a drag every now and then when I needed it. Well, I went right back like blazing saddles.

Proverbs 6:2-3 (NIV) says, "If you have been trapped by what you said, ensnared by the words of your mouth, then do this, my son, to free yourself, since you have fallen into your neighbor's hands: Go and humble yourself; press your plea with your neighbor!"

I had told everyone, and I mean everyone! I felt like I had to tell them the truth. Jesus didn't fail; it was me, and I was sorry. I felt like such a failure all because I couldn't stop smoking. I was even considering leaving Aglow, as much as I loved it, because our meetings were so long, I was in a cold sweat by the time we closed.

Then, someone told me of a prayer meeting in Hammonton where people were being delivered from the habit. I traveled to this meeting. When it was my turn, the Reverend had me jump up and down on my cigarettes and crush them in the Name of Jesus. You name it, I did it. He had laid his hands on me and was praying and the whole time I was thinking it was all right because I have another pack in the glove compartment.

What St. Paul said in Romans 7:19 sure is true: "For the good that I would I do not: but the evil which I would not, that I do." I really wanted to quit, but I wanted to smoke at the same time.

My father also smoked. One night we all went to a Full Gospel Businessmen's dinner. My Mom and Dad and Boo and I. My folks had never been to any of these types of meetings.

Even before the speaker began, he called my Daddy up front. He didn't even get to lay his hand on my father, when he went out in the Spirit. That did it; I knew for sure now that was real. My Dad never heard of being slain, never saw it, and on top of that, he had a bad heart. No way in his two-hundred-dollar suit would he fall on the floor in this restaurant in front of everyone if it wasn't God's Power.

When he got up and returned to the table, my father handed me his cigarettes and lighter and not in a quiet voice, believe me, tells me he'll never smoke again. Oh, great. At that moment I felt like the prodigal son's brother. Not fair; I was trying so hard to get delivered. I found out later that was my problem. I then decided to quit trying. I smoked and Jesus still loved me. Couldn't you?? Please!

Months went by and one day I was over at Barbara's house. (Remember the crazy lady who prayed in tongues, of all things?) There were three of us there and God's Presence was so strong. Barb asked me what I wanted God to do for me. I almost didn't ask about the smoking for fear of failing again. Don't you let Satan do that to you! You knock, and you'll find the door *will* be opened for you.

We prayed the Lord would take away the desire for cigarettes. After we prayed, I realized I really meant it. I didn't want to smoke any longer. Just like Peter when he got out of that boat and walked on the water, my act of faith was to follow that prayer. I had just bought a Lady Buxton cigarette case for six dollars and fifty cents. (Remember cheap Gwen who is now a tight steward?) This time I didn't remove the cigarettes and throw them away in Jesus' Name. I threw out the case and all. As soon as that brand new case hit the trash, I knew I really was delivered and that I would never smoke again. Glory to God! Every time I would think about a cigarette, I'd say in my mind, "Praise God — I'll never want another cigarette, and I'll never smoke again."

The battle is in the mind, believe me. Whatever you are fighting, even today, starts in your mind. That is why the Word of God in Romans 12:2 admonishes us: "And be not conformed to this world: but be ye transformed by the renewing of your mind, that ye may prove what is that good, and acceptable, and perfect, will of God."

Don't entertain thoughts of temptation. Think on things of a good report (Philippians 4:8). I want to tell you all of my good report: the first month of my deliverance from cigarettes, I lost four pounds and had no withdrawal of any kind.

Soon after this, the Board of a local Women's Aglow asked me to speak at a breakfast meeting. I found my gift from God. I loved it, and I was sure this was to be my ministry.

I figured the cards and calls would start coming in now. I waited and waited. For two years I waited, and I allowed it to die. I wanted it too much. I needed to let it go. If it was God's will for me, He would resurrect it in the Spirit, and I would have nothing to do with it. Don't hold on too tightly; you can harm yourself.

Since that time God has been opening doors for me to speak and to minister. I want to share just a few things that I hope will help you and that I have learned.

A few years ago a pastor called me. He was taking care of three cute little Methodist churches (He was a circuit preacher), and he wanted me to go to each one and share my testimony and then to another church for a revival he was having. I was delighted. Everything was fine at the churches until we hit the revival.

I took a girlfriend along with me that night. We met the pastor of this church — a woman (no comment). My friend expressed her thanks that we could come and share our born-again experience with her people. Her reply was, "Oh, you're one of them."

During a dinner, which preceded the revival, I found out this lady pastor would chart your stars and read your palm in her study; I realized this was not good, but I didn't see the power of darkness right at that moment.

When it came time to enter the sanctuary to begin our service, she stayed out in the foyer. When I took the pulpit, all I could see was this pastor marching back and forth, back and forth. Spiritual thing that I was, I never prayed or bound these forces of darkness. The entire time I was speaking, I felt as though I was choking. I'll never go anywhere now that I don't take authority over Satan and his laborers. You make sure you do the same.

On the lighter side, I was asked to speak at a Women's Club dinner recently. I was told when invited that these ladies were older, more like my Grand-Moms. That's okay with me, as the Gospel is for old and young alike.

As I sat down to break bread with these women at their covered dish supper, one lady at my table began to tell me how expensive these dinners are to her and how they always make her bring the meat. "Four dollars for chicken legs, have you ever?" At this point, I felt sorry for her. I asked her how often they have these suppers. Her reply: "Once a year." I really had to laugh.

During the time I was preaching, one lady, eighty-seven, got up. She didn't move too fast. I had at this time lost the audience, so I figured I would wait until she left. I mean, we all knew where she was going. Ten minutes later back she came. With a smile on my face, I waited until she sat down. Someone must have asked her if she was all right. Her reply, nice and loud, was, "Too many beans!" We all ended up laughing. I think after that I can handle anything.

Have a good time for and with God, won't you!

CHAPTER VI

Who Will Take
a 32-Year-Old Orphan?

It has been a delight to share my joys with you, but I have also had some very sorrowful times. Remember the verses, "Sorrowful, yet always rejoicing?" (II Corinthians 6:10).

When my parents were saved about a year or so, maybe a little longer, and my Dad was an usher at church, (I was so very proud of him), on Mother's Day 1978, my mother called me from the hospital. She was not sick; this time it was my father.

They had been with us in the Sunday morning service. Sitting at their kitchen table later, my father had a stroke. Even as he fell to the floor, he didn't want my Mom to call the ambulance. With what strength he had left, he knocked the phone from her hand. She did get help, and as soon as she could, she called me.

I rushed over there that night not knowing what I would find or even what I could do. It was a massive stroke that left his entire right side paralyzed, and he could no longer speak. That night they didn't know if he would live. They let us stay with him. The next few days are a blur in my mind. They said he would live, but they didn't know how much of his damage was permanent. Would he ever speak again? Only time would tell.

The next few weeks were horrible for me and I'm sure they were tearing my Mom's heart apart. You see it on television, but you cannot believe that in the late 1970's in modern America, the older folks are not being taken care of.

Seated in what looked like a huge high chair, with no return yet of anything on his right side and no speech, my Dad would be placed in the halls alone, bent over, helpless. Though sixty, he looked ninety. Were these really his golden years?

My Mom and I would be there every mealtime to help him. Have you ever tried to open one of those food containers with only one hand? It would be left on his tray — the tray delivered

— that's all. At almost two hundred dollars a day, was this really happening?

After six weeks they transferred him to a rehabilitation hospital to begin therapy. He still couldn't do anything for himself at all. My proud father — what a terrible thing to happen to a man full of love and life just weeks ago.

At the Rehab hospital they gave him a brace for his right leg. He had enough strength to throw his hip out and the leg would move with a cane on his left arm. His right arm was in a sling. After three months I saw him walk for the first time.

I cried as I watched him struggle just to take a few hard-earned steps. Could this really be my Daddy who to me was so big and strong?

I remember when he put his T-shirt on for himself. They had taught him how to hold it with his teeth. I watched as somehow he finally got it over his head. When his head popped through that hole, his face lit up like a Christmas tree. He worked so hard for something we daily take for granted.

Weeks passed. Still his only words which he could say were, "Good, Lord, and Oh, Boy." This was harder on all of us than any of the other physical handicaps. He could not communicate with us.

They got him a card with the alphabet and a pointer to spell his words. That just about drove him crazy. He never was one to write letters because he couldn't spell well. Every time my mother and I would ask him to spell what he wanted, the only letters he would bother to point to were N and O. "No!" Then he'd smile. He was like a little boy at times. We would try again. This time he'd be smiling even before he hit the letter N.

One afternoon I had gone to a small prayer meeting with Terri (the lady with the fleece). A man around 65 began to testify how years ago he had been in a mine shaft that collapsed — breaking and crushing both his legs. They got him to a hospital and X-rayed his legs. The whole time he was yelling to go home, so the elders could anoint him with oil for his healing. Against the doctor's orders, they checked him out and took him home.

They never even got the stretcher inside his house. Right there on his front porch they laid hands on him, anointed him with oil, and God healed him. He jumped right off that stretcher and started dancing in the Holy Ghost right there.

I looked over at Terri and she looked at me. I believed. I mean I really believed. We left with a bottle of oil and went to anoint my father in the Name of the Lord, according to James 5:14-15. Terri carried around with her a little book with all the Scriptures on healing. As she began to read them to my Daddy, he started crying.

Faith comes by hearing the Word of God. We were moving in faith, and we wanted Daddy full of faith. We asked him if he believed God was going to heal him. As he shook his head, yes, yes, and said, "Good Lord," we laid our hands on him and prayed.

We told him in the Name of Jesus to get up! I was expecting him up at any second. He didn't move!! I don't share this with you because I don't believe in Divine Healing — I most certainly DO believe. I can't explain that afternoon to you. Someone related a story to try to help me.

There's a young man on a motorcycle about to jump a gully. He asks if you believe he can do it. "Sure do; go ahead. I believe you can." He then tells you, "All right, you believe — jump on the back!"

I pray if you have ever felt disappointed, this will help you, and you will want to get to the place where you jump on the bike *before* he ever asks. I do!

It had been months now — my Daddy was still in the Rehab hospital. The time was approaching for him to come home.

A friend suggested my mother get a routine checkup because she needed to be strong to help lift my Dad in and out of his wheelchair.

Before she even went to the doctor, I felt the Lord speak to me. He told me He had prepared a mansion for her, and He was going to take her. (Now wait a minute. It's my father who is sick. My Mom's in perfect health. And yet, I know that still small voice.)

You may have trouble agreeing with me or even believing it was God. I said in the very beginning I would share with you in truth — honesty. As I have studied the Scriptures, I have seen where God has told many that it was their time. He told Moses and Joseph. In the New Testament, Paul says in II Timothy 4:6-7, "For I am now ready to be offered, and the time of my departure is at hand. I have fought a good fight, I have finished my course, I have kept the faith."

In II Peter 1:14 we read, "Knowing that shortly I must put off this my tabernacle, even as our Lord Jesus Christ hath showed me" (this latter verse referring to John 21:18-19). Even Peter was instructed by the Lord concerning his death and the timing of it.

Perhaps one reason the Lord spoke this to me was because of my father's condition. Because he couldn't talk, I could not ask him what my mother wanted when she died. Did they have wills, etc.?

As it turned out, I never had to really discuss all this with either one of them.

It was October 1978 when the report came back that there was a spot on my mother's lung. In November they put Mom in the hospital. I put my Daddy's bed in our dining room. He was able to be with us while they were testing my mother.

On Thanksgiving Day they let her come home and told her she did not need surgery. As we sat around my turkey table, I knew this was my last Thanksgiving with my mother. She prayed and gave God thanks that day for letting her come home without another operation in her life.

When I saw the doctor, he told me she had a large malignant tumor on her kidney that was inoperable. He gave her six months to live. This was around Christmastime of '78.

Mother was now tired all the time. Even though it was the birth of our Savior and cause for celebration, as I looked at my Daddy in his wheelchair and my Mom on the couch, my heart was breaking.

Inside of me there was a battle raging; the Christian woman was saying — "Oh, to see Jesus!" (II Corinthians 5:8: ". . . to be absent from the body, and to be present with the Lord.") and yet the little girl inside me was saying, "Mommy, please don't leave me."

It was time to let all my Mom's relatives know what was happening. I called my uncle and my mother's three sisters, the nuns. They were going to come down as soon as they heard. I had not told my Dad yet. I knew he would know if they all came rushing in. I tried to explain this, but somehow they felt I was keeping them away because we were no longer Catholics.

What they didn't realize is there is one Lord, one faith. The Jesus my mother believed in was the same Jesus she loved as a child; only now, she knew Him.

They all did come down, and I was able to keep my Dad calm. The house felt like death. I decided to take my aunts to the Boardwalk for awhile. We no sooner got there than I was told, with clenched fists, that if I didn't bury my mother Catholic, none of them would come.

I just stood there with my back against the railing, tears rolling out from under my sunglasses. At that moment I needed the love and compassion of Jesus. I needed the mercy of God through them. (I think of Stephen, the first martyr, in Acts 7:60, crying out, "Lord, lay not this sin to their charge." Indeed, they did not know what they were doing.)

Within a short time, my Mom's condition went downhill. We went through the various treatments . . . by the beginning of May, however, at fifty-nine years of age, my mother was once again completely bedridden. This time I wasn't six years old, and I wanted to love and care for her.

My brother Dirk, his wife, Rose, and their two children drove up from Florida. They were going to stay and help take care of my parents. Dirk is a fisherman so he sold his boat and came up here. I will thank God always for Rosie, my sister-in-law, for being willing to drop everything, rent out their home, and come and stay at my folks'.

My parents had been married thirty-seven years, and we weren't going to separate them now. We changed their dining room into a room for Mom. The American Cancer Society got us a hospital bed, and we had things running as smooth as possible.

My father knew she was sick, but I don't think in the beginning he knew how serious it was. Now a year after his stroke and he still could not talk. That, by far, was the most painful thing about his condition. I remember telling the Lord one night, "Wouldn't I ever hear him call my name again this side of heaven?"

A few days later I had him on the back porch for some fresh air. Through the screen door, as clear as a bell, he called my name, "Gwen." I went running to him as he pointed for me to get the mail from the mailman. I did indeed hear him call me by name. (Thank You, Jesus!)

It must have been so hard on him to have lost his manhood; now Rosie and I were caring for him. Once he got a birthday card in the mail with ten dollars in it. He wouldn't part with that money for anything. Since his stroke, he didn't have a wallet or keys anymore. For days, though, he would keep that ten dollar bill in his pocket and every night, as I got him ready for bed, he'd put it on his dresser and with a strong, "Oh, Boy," I knew it had better be there in the morning.

One afternoon all of us, including Mom, felt like "subs." As Dirk went out to pick up the order, out of my Dad's pocket came his birthday money and once again, he treated us, as he had done so often in the past.

Mom was now in great pain. We gave her all the medicine and yet she was still suffering. I would hear her pray at night for Jesus to help her not to complain. She'd tell Him she loved Him so. I was on a cot at the end of her bed, just crying softly. I cried on and off in those months, but Jesus was so real and so strong in me.

Every time I needed to make a decision, He would guide and direct me. One time, when my Mom was back in the hospital, the Lord led her to write down what kind of service she wanted as a memorial. She gave it to me in the event she went home to heaven. If her family didn't understand, she would still love them.

This was such a hard time for me; it seemed sickness and death were all around us. Daddy woke up one morning with his leg really swollen. We had to take him to the hospital — he had phlebitis. Mom is dying of cancer and now Dad is back in the hospital.

By this time the cancer had gone to Mom's brain. When I looked at her sometimes, I knew she wasn't there. She didn't know me at times. She'd think we were little girls and I was her sister. We would laugh, and I'd go into the kitchen and cry and cry. It was then, however, that the terrible pain stopped for her. For that, I am so thankful. It was June when Dad found out he had phlebitis. On Father's Day I took him a box of chocolates.

I was about to comb his hair when he jerked back his head and began yelling, "Oh, Boy." He always liked to look nice; I couldn't figure out what was wrong until I looked at his head. All the way across the back of his head were stitches. He couldn't talk to tell me what happened. Why didn't someone call me? How could this happen?

I later found out that he was put on a portable toilet. With his side paralyzed, he fell off when left alone, and cracked his head wide open on the radiator. It took twenty stitches.

Without Christ, this all would have been too much for me. I have found His Word to be 100 percent true. When I am weakest, He is strong. His strength in me was enough even for me to forgive those who allowed this to happen.

Mother was much worse now. I was so glad Daddy came home soon after the stitches were removed. He knew now it was really bad, but at the beginning of July, he knew she was about to die. Had God told him as He did me?

For a few days Daddy just sat by mother's bed, patting her hand with such love and devotion. He could talk to say good-bye, but he wanted her to know he was there all the time. He would just sit in his wheelchair and cry and cry.

Since the cancer was now in her brain, she saw him as well and whole and would talk to him as if everything was fine.

The day before she died, my pastor's son had stopped over to see her. She awoke clear as a bell. She hadn't been this sound in her mind for a long time. She knew me as her daughter and told me how much she loved me. I was able to tell her how I loved her, too. We hugged each other and once again I was crying.

Then she asked me if I saw Jesus. "He's over there (pointing next to my pastor's son). He always comes with that gentleman." Right after she said that, she went to sleep. I knew she was soon to see Jesus, but God was so good to me to allow me to be there and hear her say it.

In Ecclesiastes 7:1 it says, "A good name is better than precious ointment; and the day of death than the day of one's birth." How many of us remember the day of our birth?

Praise God, though, we'll know the day of our death for we will see our Jesus.

The next day I was at the house all day and left in the early evening. Dirk and Rosie were such a blessing; I'll be grateful for them all my life. That night, after everyone had gone to bed, I began to cry — really cry. "God, I don't want my Mommy to die." "Lord, please don't let my Mommy die." I knew I was feeling sorry for myself. This pity wasn't pleasing to God. I chose to stop and to start to thank God for His wonderful goodness to me and my family.

I praised Him for Jesus, for my parents' salvation, for Dirk and Rosie being here. I just offered that sacrifice of praise. I started singing songs of praise. It was then as I sang, I knew my mother had died. The phone rang with Rosie confirming what I already knew in my spirit. It's one thing to think you're ready and another to be ready when it actually comes.

I had a twenty minute ride. All the way over I kept singing the chorus from "Great Is Thy Faithfulness." It was July 4th — a day of independence. I did want to be independent, yet I still wanted to depend on God and His Faithfulness.

"Great is Thy Faithfulness, Great is Thy Faithfulness, Morning by Morning new mercies I see; All I have needed Thy hand hath provided — Great is Thy Faithfulness, Lord, unto me!"

I walked in, not knowing how I would react when I saw my Mom's body. All at once I knew the Bible is true in its entirety. I was just a tent. It's really true: to be absent from the body is to be present with the Lord. I knew my mother was with Jesus and that really gave me comfort because one day I'll be with Jesus, and I'll see her again.

I was afraid that when I told my Daddy in the morning that he would have a heart attack right then and there and I would lose him, too. We gave him pills for his nerves and then told him. It almost broke my heart.

We had a beautiful memorial for her — all the arrangements the way she wanted them to be. My Mom was the youngest of nine children and none of her family came that day. As I was thinking on that hurt and their staying away because of tradition, the Lord had a friend give me a poem she had written which I believe with all my heart to be inspired:

I asked the Lord, the other day
For a word of comfort we could say
To help you through a time of sorrow
When grief will lessen with the morrow
We'll try to help you share this grief

Perhaps a word brings some relief
We pray God's peace upon your clan
Since your Mom went to the Promised Land
With Jesus now, all pain is gone.
She'll praise her Saviour, for eternity long
We realize she'll be sorely missed
But now she dwells in heavenly bliss
For Jesus is the only way
To reach the place where night is day!
A time to live, a time to die
So dry those tears, no need to cry
Our loved one is without a care
Some day we'll meet her over there!

I was deeply moved by this poem and after the service, I read it back at Mom's house. Somehow I knew she'd love it, too.

I didn't know what the future would hold for my Father. Dirk and Rosie would one day have to return to Florida. Then what? I couldn't put him in a nursing home. Move in with me?

Two weeks later, my Dad fell. With his cane and brace he could get around a little. Since Mom was gone, he was getting so weak. He would work so hard at his therapy before Mom got sick, to please her. Now he wouldn't even try. I just knew he felt he had nothing now to live for.

I thought he broke his hip that night. I couldn't get him off the kitchen floor. The harder I tried to pick him up, the harder he laughed. At ten o'clock at night I began running around his neighborhood, looking for a man to pick him up.

He wouldn't let me call for a doctor, but in the morning he could not move or get out of bed for the pain. Once again, I am following an ambulance.

After they took X-rays of his hip, the nurse said I could go behind the curtain and sit with him. The doctors, however, didn't know I was back there. (Remember now, my mother had only been dead two weeks.) Her doctor's name was Dr. Korey. He deals only in cancer. As I sat back there, I heard the doctors say, "George Prague, *cancer* — right hip. Call Dr. Korey."

This was almost more than I could handle. I went running out of the emergency room, crying. I let out one big yell and went back in. My mind was racing. I had seen Mom suffer so much. Now him. I never said to the Lord, "This is too much!" or "Why us?" That day, however, I said, "Is there much more?" I no sooner said that when I saw a born-again nurse I knew from church on her way over to me. She cried for me that day. God's Word tells us to rejoice with those who rejoice and weep with those who weep. Everyone wants to rejoice, but we know those who in love will weep with us and for us. Just be sensitive to those with needs.

Later, after a few weeks of testing, we did find out it wasn't cancer after all. Dad had a deterioration from not using his hip in fourteen months since his stroke.

A brain scan did reveal a blood clot on his brain. Dad wanted the surgery. They even said his speech might return.

Dad had beautiful hair and they were coming to shave it all off before the surgery. I kidded him that he was going to look just like a walrus with a bald head and his big handle bar moustache. His "Oh Boy!" rang out as I left his room.

Daddy had a bad heart and in my heart I didn't know if he would live through that operation. The doctor warned me. Still, I signed and gave my consent. It was only a month before I had lost my Mom.

Dirk and I were together in the surgical waiting room when I read the following passage in Isaiah 46:4 "And even to your old age I am He; and even to hoar hairs will I carry you: I have made, and I will bear; even I will carry, and will deliver you." I knew right at that moment my father would live."

As soon as the surgery was over, I was permitted to go into the Intensive Care Unit and see him. Next to his bed was a small brown paper bag, much like my children use for school lunches. My father's name was written on it — it was stapled closed. Since it was in a paper bag, I figured it wasn't anything sterile, so I opened it, only to find all his grey hair in there. Okay, Lord, I got the message!

Daddy seemed to be doing a little better, or was it because I wanted it so badly?

My parents had been married for thirty-seven years and during that time they had prayed every day that they would die together. I used to think that was sentimental. Now I was keenly aware of God answering prayers.

One night I prayed that if they were not to be separated any longer and indeed my father was to die, the Lord would let me know. I wanted to say goodbye to him. I wasn't there with my mother when she died. Even though I got to tell my mother how much I loved her, I wanted to be with my father.

I was on a fast this one week in August because I had a speaking engagement in Toms River. I was on the fourth day of my fast when I took Dad some macaroni salad.

As I sat there with him, the Holy Spirit spoke this scripture to my mind Philippians 1:21 "For me to live is Christ, and to die is gain." I looked at my Dad. How could he even live as Christ? He can't walk or talk. Is to die gain? I felt the Lord say to me, "Gwen, to die is gain. Say goodbye to your father." I sat there and reasoned away what the Lord had said.

I stayed after visiting hours just to be sure he was all right. I kissed him goodnight and left. As I passed the nurses' station, I told them to call me when my father turns, no matter what hour it is. They looked at me strangely and told me he was doing much better. "Just call me, please."

In my car I began thanking God that He was going to take him to heaven. I praised Him for even now preparing his mansion. I just would not have done that in the flesh. I knew it was the prompting of the Holy Spirit.

As I walked in the front door, I told Boo that tonight Daddy was going to heaven — that the Lord was coming for him. Boo looked at me rather strangely and said, "Honey, your mother just died. You're just upset." Though I went to bed early, I laid out my clothes and waited for the phone to ring. When it rang, I knew it was the hospital; Dad had taken a turn for the worse. I should come there immediately.

I started praying for the Lord to keep him alive until I got there. I just had to be able to say goodbye to him. "Oh, Jesus, let him live until I get there, please."

The scene at the hospital was one I'll not forget. It seemed like tons of people were around him. The crash cart, nurses, and doctors all were doing what they could. One was beating him on the chest, another banging him. They wouldn't let me in. Didn't they know I had to say goodbye?

Minutes (which seemed like hours) later, the doctor came out and told me there wasn't anything more they could do. He was alive, but they knew he was dying, but then again, so did I. I told the doctor I believed the Lord was keeping him alive so I could say goodbye. Wouldn't he please let me in?

I went into that room that night in the Presence and Power of God. For the very first time in all my life I didn't care what other people thought about me. For some reason doctors and lawyers have always intimidated me — those with a high degree of education. I realize now every man needs Jesus. He didn't come for rich or poor, those with college degrees or those without. He came for all humanity to bring us back into fellowship with God that we lost when Adam fell.

I walked in, looked right into my Daddy's eyes, and told him how very much I loved him and that I missed Mommy and to tell her I love her and for him to go now with Jesus — that I would see them both at the Resurrection.

The nurses in that room began to cry. I knelt down by his bed and began to pray for him. I had said my goodbyes and given him all my love; now I asked Jesus to take him. When I had ended my prayer, as I got up, I noticed all the staff had left the room. I was alone with my Daddy. He wasn't dead, so I began to speak to him.

I assured him when he received his new body, he'd be able once again to walk and talk — that there are no stroke victims in heaven, no cancer, no sickness, nor disease. "Oh, Daddy, go with Jesus into life and total health."

For the last fourteen months I'd seen him suffer. I wanted him at peace, yet I didn't want to let him go. He was having a hard time breathing. What should I do? I began to sing. I knew deep down inside my spirit that if I was to sing, "Great Is Thy Faithfulness," the song God gave me when my mother died, he would go. I didn't want to lose him, and yet I had no right to keep him here.

Finally, in love and the peace of God, I, with worship in my heart, sang, "Great is Thy Faithfulness, Lord unto me." At that very moment, Daddy crossed over into Glory, and for him, I was glad. I kissed him for the last time this side of heaven, covered him as gently as I could, and went out into the hall.

Because I was singing, there was a crowd of people outside his door. I had the opportunity to witness to a few of them the reality of Jesus.

"Jesus said unto her, I am the resurrection, and the life: he that believeth in Me, though he were dead, yet shall he live: And whosoever liveth and believeth in Me shall never die. Believest thou this?" John 11:25-26.

I believed this with all my heart. In all of Scripture this is one of my favorite verses. I was always afraid of death and dying. Even in my twenties, I would ask people all the time if I died, would they please come to my funeral. I wanted Boo to find an undertaker who would let me have my eyes open at my own viewing. I had a fear of dying that I know now was from Satan. There are only two choices we have: God or Satan. When I was afraid, I was still serving Satan at that time in my life.

One day Hebrews 2:14-15 really set me free from the fear of death and the fear of dying. How I thank God for His Word! If you are fearful of death, let the Spirit of God set you free through these verses: "Forasmuch then as the children are partakers of flesh and blood, he also himself likewise took part of the same; that through death he might destroy him that had the power of death, that is, the devil; And deliver them who through fear of death were all their lifetime subject to bondage."

I was no longer in bondage to my fear of dying after I received the Word into my heart. That night I actually saw my father die, and I knew again how true the Word of God is. That must be one more reason why it says that the Word is living. As we go through life living one day at a time, the Word will live with us.

With his cane and personal belongings, I headed for my car. Each time I looked down at that cane, something in my heart knew he was walking on streets of gold.

I didn't sleep all that night, and I decided not to break my fast. I knew in my heart that the Lord would do great things at the meeting.

No one in Toms River knew about my father's death when I got there to speak and to minister. A lady came up and she had a Scripture for me: Joshua 1:9: "Have not I commanded thee? Be strong and of a good courage; be not afraid, neither be thou dismayed: for the Lord thy God is with thee whithersoever thou goest."

I knew the Lord was with me. The Bible says that when you fast in secret, the Lord will reward you openly. I was about to receive a reward I'll remember always.

As I began to share my testimony with these ladies, they were all having a good time, laughing. When I told them my mother died last month at the age of fifty-five and now my father had died last night, a holy silence fell upon that place. I asked them if they were ready to meet God. The Holy Spirit just fell on us. All over that room women stood to receive Christ and become right in their hearts toward God. It was like a revival. I don't have an exact count, but over eighteen women were born again that evening. Many were filled with the Spirit of God. I prayed and ministered for over two hours that night. I didn't want anyone to leave with a need.

Jesus seemed to be saying to me that unless a kernel falls into the ground and dies, it produces no new life. I was rejoicing over all the additions into the kingdom of God that evening. "Sorrowful, yet always rejoicing."

My pastor had a beautiful memorial service for my father. For the first time, I heard the words to "Great Is Thy Faithfulness." Our youth pastor sang it; I want to share this verse with you. Didn't God pick just the songs I needed!

"Pardon for sin and a peace that endureth, Thine own dear presence to cheer and to guide, Strength for today and bright hope for tomorrow — Blessings all mine, with ten thousand beside!"

In closing this difficult chapter for me to write, let me say to you: You are never really dead as long as someone is left to remember you. And when there's no one left to remember you, it doesn't matter because it means you are all together again.

Though God had been with me all along, all of a sudden I realized I had no parents. In just six short weeks, I was alone — like an orphan at thirty-two years of age. I knew Jesus lived in me and I knew all the Scriptures I should take comfort in, but my parents were really gone.

Dirk and Rosie were still here. We had a big house to empty, etc. As I was going through some papers and letters of my Mom's, I realized that no longer was anything personal. It didn't seem fair that I had to read and sort through all these things that meant so much to her.

About a month after they died, Women's Aglow was having a weekend retreat. Boo talked me into going. He said I'd had a very hard year with so much pain and sickness, it would do me good to get away from everything and spend time alone with God.

That weekend was to change my life! When I arrived, we were given a schedule of times the speaker would minister and what workshops would be available.

On the bottom of the sheet, a workshop had been cancelled and in its place there was a workshop on Grief. I knew where I was going. I felt like grief was all around me. I knew I wasn't mourning like the world, but something was still wrong in me. What was it?

This workshop was taught by a young woman whose daughter had died of leukemia. She was sharing her grief and sorrow as well as trying to show us what God's Word said on this subject.

She made a statement that hit me so hard, it was like a ton of bricks. She said she never really was mad at God for her daughter's death, but she had a hard time forgiving her daughter for leaving her.

I knew that was what was wrong with me. Even though neither one of them wanted to die, they were gone, and I hadn't forgiven them. I didn't know until then I even needed to do such a thing.

I began to cry right there in the workshop; I couldn't seem to stop. They laid hands on me and prayed and I got control, but I wanted them to talk and counsel with me. Right then, they broke for lunch. Who can eat at a time like this? Evidently, they could. My composure returned and I joined my other friends in the cafeteria. The menu was grilled cheese and chicken noodle soup — one of my favorites. Then again, what isn't my favorite? (We'll get into that later in this book.) I was so upset, I couldn't eat. I left there and wanted to be alone with God.

I returned to my cabin, and I threw a fit. (I am not kidding!) I beat the pillow, cried and yelled. It seemed so unfair; they came to Jesus and now they were dead. I was soon to realize I was mad at God. Not only did I need to forgive God and have Him forgive me, but I needed to forgive my parents and really let them go.

Even today I see people who have lost someone they loved years ago, and they can hardly talk about it. There are others who won't go to certain places because it may cause them a memory and pain. Others keep the room just as it was. This is not freedom. It's bondage!

I was determined I wasn't going to leave that cabin until I heard from God. One time I wanted to hear from God. I did everything this little book told me to do. I got quiet, bound the voice of satan, willed my own thoughts dead, and waited. The inner voice I heard said Romans 18:8. I really got excited. God had spoken to me. I ran down to get my Bible. I just knew this was going to be good. Suddenly I discovered there are only sixteen chapters in Romans. There is no Romans 18:8. Ever since I helped God that time, I have been very cautious when a verse will drop into my head..

On my knees that afternoon I heard in my mind: John 16:20 & 22. Slowly I got my Bible. Was this even in the Bible? Not only was it in there, it was for me: "Verily, verily I say unto you, That ye shall weep and lament, but the world shall rejoice: and ye shall be sorrowful, but your sorrow shall be turned into joy. And ye now therefore have sorrow: but I will see you again, and your heart shall rejoice, and your joy no man taketh from you."

I asked God to cleanse me and forgive me and then I did something very hard: I forgave my parents for dying and leaving me. I was again filled with the joy of the Lord, and just like my Jesus said, no man has or can take it from me.

CHAPTER VII

Tick Fever To
Mountain-Moving Faith

After the death of my parents in 1979, I didn't know what 1980 would hold for me. There was still sadness every time I had to go over to their empty house.

Dirk, Rosie, and their children went back to Florida. I didn't feel as though I had any family left. Well, at least Boo had his family close by.

In March 1980 they found a malignant lump in my father-in-law's throat. What a rotten disease cancer is! I knew it wasn't from God. We were really concerned because he was seventy-three years old and had never received Christ as his Savior.

Boo's sister, Viki, and her husband were believers, but Connie, my father-in-law, wasn't saved. Boo and I began to pray together for him. We both knew it is appointed unto man once to die and then the judgment. We knew he wasn't ready.

My husband was on strike and this one afternoon he felt led to go see his Dad. My father-in-law had been having cobalt treatments and was now home from the hospital. As Boo left, I began to intercede. I knew Connie was going to be saved and sure enough, my husband had the honor and pleasure of leading his own father to the Lord. The angels in heaven were rejoicing and so were we.

He died in August 1980 — almost a year to the day since my Dad's death. It seemed death was all around us, yet we knew we had the light and life of God within us. Seventy-four years is a long life. It's just a shame he didn't live it for Jesus. Just like the good thief on the cross saying to Jesus, "Lord, remember me when you come into your kingdom," and the Lord took him to paradise, it is never too late to receive Jesus. If you haven't by now, don't put it off any longer. God loves you! He really does!

As you can see from all that I have shared, I wasn't having

healing lines when I went out to minister. I felt my faith was really low at this point in time.

I would begin to grow in my faith-walk in the near future, but first the Lord needed to touch me in a real way.

Long about June 1980 there was a large Christian convention in Pittsburgh and Boo said I could go. The Lord really was changing me. I wanted to go, but I didn't want to leave my family. Eventually, I did go.

One evening after the services a lady came into our room for prayer. It turned out she had cancer in the very same area as did my mother. She was my Mom's age, and this was just too much for me. I didn't want any doubt or unbelief from me to hinder their prayer, so I thought I would just sit in the corner and pray in the Spirit. I heard one lady say to her, "This sickness is not unto death." I thought that was great. I didn't remember anyone ever quoting that. I wanted to ask her where that was in the Scripture, but I thought if I did, they would think I didn't read my Bible, so I would wait until I got home and then look it up.

Even when I got home, I shared this with Boo. Before I even had time to dig it out, there it was in my Bible reading the very next evening.

John 11:4, "When Jesus heard that, (Lazarus was sick) He said, This sickness is not unto death, but for the glory of God, that the Son of God might be glorified thereby."

I didn't know then that at a later time I would need this Scripture to save my life. I underlined it, as we do, and went on with my life.

In a few days I awoke with a small lump in the middle of my back. It was small so I didn't really pay any attention to it.

However, I didn't feel well that day. That night I ran a very high fever. During the next day, my condition grew worse and worse. This little bump was now all red and the size of a dime. My fever got so high that night, my teeth were chattering. In the morning I hurt all over. Every muscle and joint hurt. What was the matter with me? I didn't remember being that sick in all my days.

Boo called from work that morning to see how I was. This little bump was now about the size of a quarter. He finally convinced me to call our doctor. As I explained all my symptoms and distress over the phone, the doctor said he would open his office early — for me to come in right away.

When I got there, he looked at my back and ran over his medical journals. Finally he found the pages he was looking for and he began to read each and every symptom of mine. At one point he even said he hadn't seen a case of this in years. (Oh, great! Leave it to me!)

He then told me I had Rocky Mountain Spotted Tick Fever. He began telling me how serious this is. Next thing I know I was at the hospital, one nurse taking my blood and the other one showing everyone my tick bite. Cute!

I was allowed to go home for total bed rest, and he would keep in touch with me. As soon as Boo found out, he came rushing home.

Even before he got there, without any medical books, I had my nose buried in the World Book. It read: Rocky Mt. Spotted Tick Fever, Fatal, serious; Fatal!- Fatal! I couldn't believe what I was reading.

There I was, flat on my back, with Boo Boo taking care of me, the house, and the children.

Ladies, if you ever feel you aren't needed or you really don't do very much, lie down for three days and you will soon see what I mean.

My fever was still very high, and I was very weak. My kids hadn't had any veggies in a couple of days. I asked Boo that night to open a can of stewed tomatoes to go with the frozen chicken you just pop in the oven. "Sure, honey," was his reply and over at our stove, I heard ever so softly, "another dirty pot." He really did a beautiful job, and I love him so.

As I laid there, I had a great deal of time to think. Was all this of the devil? Was it of God? I soon came to the conclusion that this was just something that happened; you know, an element of the world.

I knew in the Old Testament that God had put diseases on people. I knew from the New Testament that many times when Jesus healed, it was because the sickness was from Satan. The woman who had the issue of blood (in Mark 5:25) — Satan had her bound twelve years even though she was a daughter of Abraham.

I knew three forces are mentioned in Scripture: God, the

Devil, and the flesh. If someone smokes three packs a day and gets lung cancer, or if you live in man-made pollution and reap the effects of no clean air, is this God's fault or the flesh (the world)?

I was to the point now that I live in the woods and a tick bit me. Is God really involved in all this? Or, did a tick get me — plain and simple?

My pastor called as I was meditating on all this that I now know as "junk meditation" on God's Word. He told me the congregation was praying for me. He had no idea what was going on in my head. He then said, "Gwen, remember, His eye is on the sparrow" (Oh, no, if it's on the sparrow, it was on the tick now, wasn't it?)

I wasn't supposed to get up. On the third day I sat up to drink my ginger ale and Boo Boo said, "It's going to be so hard to raise these kids alone." Still in my mind were the words, "Fatal. Fatal." I started crying, "I don't want to die. I am dying. I don't want to die," and out of my mouth from my Spirit-man with great force came, "This sickness is not unto death." As I spoke the Word of God, the fever broke, and I knew I was healed. God had sent His Word and healed me. (Psalm 107:20)

When the doctor called and I began to explain how I was healed, the man thought the fever had fried my brain. Nevertheless, he sent me back to the hospital for blood work. The results from the first set were back and confirmed that I did indeed have the Fever.

When this new sample of blood came back, there wasn't a trace of any infection of any kind. Glory to Jesus!!

I began to dig into the scriptures to see about healing. There are only two ways we can read the Bible. One is to see what God is saying, and the other is to back up what we believe already.

I knew I didn't have faith for my healing after all I'd been through, which is no excuse, but I used it anyhow. So, I came to the conclusion I was healed because of the faith of those who were praying for me and because of the power in the Word of God. I then found a scripture to agree with me: Matthew 9:1-2: "And He entered into a ship, and passed over, and came into His own city. And, behold, they brought to Him a man sick of the palsy, lying on a bed: and Jesus seeing *their* faith said unto the sick of the palsy: Son, be of good cheer; thy sins be forgiven thee." In verse 6, "But that ye may know that the Son of man hath power on earth to forgive sins, (then saith He to the sick of the palsy,) Arise, take up thy bed, and go unto thine house." Here Jesus healed him because of the faith of his friends, and he even got his sins forgiven.

For almost a year I studied only the Scriptures on the blind man who didn't even know who Jesus was, yet he got healed. I stayed away from any and all Scriptures that had to do with me or my faith.

I didn't read any books on Faith. I read all I could find on Paul's thorn. People who were into positive confession were making me crazy. (There's a good confession!)

One lady whose father was an alcoholic sat at my kitchen table and said, "He's not an alcoholic. He's not an alcoholic, but he's going to be delivered!" Well, if he's not an alcoholic, deliverance from what? I didn't understand this. They would ask, "How's your Mom?" "Really sick," I would say. All I'd get then was, "Don't confess it."

Then one morning I read Mark 11:23, "For verily I say unto you, That whosoever shall say unto this mountain, Be thou removed, and be thou cast into the sea; and shall not doubt in his heart, but shall believe that those things which he saith shall come to pass; he shall have whatsoever he saith."

Oh, my, didn't this look like I could have what I say? Is there a truth in what they were saying?

During this time no one had shown me any Scripture. What I needed was for someone to open to me the Word of God. If there's a teaching going on in the Body where you fellowship, get into the Word and receive your truth from the Holy Spirit. He was sent to remind you of all the things Jesus said.

I had been to a picnic where these gals were discussing this teaching on positive confession. It was Brother So and So said this, and Brother So and So said that. I never heard them say even once, Jesus said or God's Word said. I was really upset. I wouldn't have listened to a tape of Brother So and So for money. (Now I buy the tapes as fast as I'm through with those I have listened to. Why?)

I found out these men were and are preaching the Word of God. This happened even in Bible days. In I Corinthians 3:4

Paul speaks of one, saying, "I am of Paul; and another, I am of Apollos." He admonishes in I Corinthians 4:6, ". . . that ye might learn in us not to think of men above that which is written, that no one of you be puffed up for one against another."

I looked again at my Bible and Mark 11:23. I wasn't going to get off that couch that morning until I understood.

First, I saw that you have to speak to the problem or situation. "Be thou removed and cast into the sea," and "Oh,praise God, my mountain's in the sea." You need to speak what you want to happen. "Be thou removed!" "Shall not doubt in his heart" — I had a hard time with this. How do you get doubt out of your heart? How do you believe something you really want to believe when you don't believe it?

The Spirit of God spoke to me and told me only faith will replace doubt in my heart. I know every man has been given the measure of faith, and I know there is a gift of faith and the fruit of the Spirit — faith. I wanted to ask God to give faith to me either as the gift of faith or to grow it (the fruit) — as I walk in love. But the Lord wanted me to learn how to move in mountain-moving faith!

I know faith comes by hearing the Word of God. The more you confess the Word, as you hear it, you will be getting more faith. As faith fills your heart, doubt and unbelief go.

"Shall believe that those things which he saith shall come to pass; he shall have whatsoever he saith." It was as if a light exploded in my head. I could finally see it for myself.

If I were confessing the Word of God out of my mouth and as I heard it, faith was growing and doubt was leaving, I would have what I was saying. When I finally got up from that couch, I discovered two hours had passed. I had been so hurt by the "confession" teaching, I think I would have sat there all day until I understood what the Holy Spirit had been wanting to show me all along. This is one reason Jesus saw to warn us to be careful what we hear.

I had even been told Proverbs 18:21, "Death and life are in the power of the tongue." Yes, that's true, but my tongue won't kill you. Just because I said my mother had cancer didn't mean I killed her. It's my life and my death that are controlled by the tongue. The Lord showed me that by my words I will be justified and by my words, condemned. I started to study Matthew 12:35-37. In verse 35a, "A good man out of the good treasure of the heart bringeth forth good things:" I kept thinking about "bringeth forth." It is true you can have what you say with your mouth. I decided then and there to speak the Word of God out of my mouth. I didn't want it just to come from my head because this passage said from your heart.

I began to fill my heart with His Word so it would come out of my mouth. Jesus said in Matthew 12:34b, ". . . for out of the abundance of the heart the mouth speaketh."

For many months for every need I would speak God's Word to my situation. I was having one problem I just didn't know how to handle.

My parents' house had been on the market almost two years. It was very depressing for me every time I had to go over there. It was cold, empty, and grey. I needed to pray before I even went in. We tried everything . . . painting, praying, lowering the price, lowering the price, lowering the price. I couldn't find a Scripture that said, "Thus saith Century 21."

We had rented it to some young fellows (a mistake) and the place was a mess. I went over to clean it up; I just stood in that empty living room crying out to God. what would it take to sell this house? What did I have to do to get God to answer my prayers. I just sobbed and cried that afternoon.

When I got home, there was a call from my real estate lady. A good deal had come in and this looked like it would sell for sure. Glory, Glory, Glory! Surely this was from God? All I need to do is get to the end of my rope, in the future, and cry and pray. Sure enough, God would answer then.

Not so: that deal fell through. I was terribly shaken. You see, there is nothing wrong with emotions, but it's faith that moves God. After that deal collapsed, I was at the end of myself. What did the Scripture say? — Your mountain can be cast into the sea. My folks' house is on the bay. Right about now I wanted it cast into the bay and at least I could ge the insurance money.

Again let me say it is faith that moves God. A few weeks later, as I sat in church on a Sunday morning, I was scanning the Bible (sorry, Pastor) and my eyes fell on John 15:7, "If ye abide in Me, and My Words abide in you, ye shall ask what ye will, and it shall be done unto you."

I knew I was abiding in God's Word, and He was abiding in me. Right then I asked for that house to sell. It said I could ask what I will and I asked. I then began to put my faith into action. I declared with my mouth the house was sold. I believed I received it when I prayed. (See Mark 11:24).

Whenever the real estate lady would call, I'd tell her not to worry. According to Mark 11:24 and John 15:7, it was sold. Now it didn't look sold, but then again if it was, I wouldn't need any faith because faith is the evidence of things not seen. I had the evidence of my faith and I knew it was sold.

It was only six weeks from that morning in church 'til we closed at settlement. I was ready to speak to any house, any mountain. Just show it to me and with faith we'll move it.

I was great with inanimate objects — those things I couldn't touch, but what about pain and sickness?

Very early one morning, around 6:45, I was going food shopping. (I don't like the crowds, so I shop while everyone is sleeping.) A well-known faith and healing preacher was about to come on the radio. I thought, "Oh, no, you don't!" As I reached for the button to turn him off, God spoke to me not to touch that dial. He made a statement that just turned me around. Of all the healing Jesus did in the New Testament, nineteen mentioned, I think, twelve out of the nineteen mention faith.

I dug into my Bible now with my eyes open, not to back me up, but to see what God has to say. I began to listen to tapes. I really wanted to believe deep down I didn't have to have any sickness. Matthew 8:16-17, "When the even was come, they brought unto Him many that were possessed with devils: and he cast out the spirits with His Word, and healed all that were sick: That it might be fulfilled which was spoken by Isaiah the prophet, saying, Himself took our infirmities, and bare our sickness." Every time I read that I would think that when He healed those people, that was the fulfillment of the Scripture.

The Spirit of God spoke to me. If Jesus fulfilled it *before the cross*, He would never have been beaten and bruised for our healing. He just would have died for our sins. Isaiah 53:5, "But He was wounded for our transgressions, He was bruised for our iniquities: the chastisement of our peace was upon Him; and with His Stripes we are healed."

Now with all my heart I believed Jesus was whipped for my healing. I still had to contend with where did sickness come from? Did God put sickness on my folks? So many people teach and believe God puts sickness on us to teach us. We may indeed learn of God's goodness through sickness, but I knew from watching, my folks' sickness didn't teach you anything. It hurt too much.

I began to listen to all the tapes I could get on healing. I needed to get the Word of God in my heart to drive out doubt and unbelief. After over thirty tapes, I still didn't have my answer when all of a sudden one tape said, "If God puts sickness on you, are you another saviour?" I realized at that moment God put sickness on Jesus. He doesn't need to put it on me if Jesus carried it for me. Now I could understand the difference between the Old Testament and the New.

In the Old Testament God put sickness and disease on people. Now He would no longer put sickness on men. Why? Because He put it on Jesus. Satan didn't put disease on Jesus. God did. Isaiah 53:4, 10, "Surely He hath borne our griefs, and carried our sorrows: yet we did esteem Him stricken, smitten of God, and afflicted . . . Yet it pleased the Lord to bruise Him; He hath put Him to grief . . ."

I finally understood that sickness is from Satan, Jesus came to heal, and by faith right then I received my healing much like I received my new birth. I believed the Word of God and I confessed it with my mouth. I Peter 2:24, "Who His own self bare our sins in His own body on the tree, that we, being dead to sins, should live unto righteousness: by Whose stripes ye were healed."

Shortly after this wonderful truth got into my spirit, I awoke with a cold. I went back to Deuteronomy 28 where it says all sickness and every disease is under the curse, even sickness not named. Well, that includes the common cold as well as cancer.

I started confessing I Peter 2:24 and Galatians 3:13, "Christ hath redeemed us from the curse of the law, being made a curse for us; for it is written, Cursed is every one that hangeth on a tree."

I told Satan to forget it. I was healed; this cold was under the curse, and I have been redeemed from the curse. I really felt rotten — sore throat, sniffles, etc., but I wasn't going to glorify the devil and disease from my mouth because if those things which I *say* are going to come to pass, they're going to be good things.

Praise the Lord, Boo never asked me how I felt or if I had a cold. You see, I can't and won't lie, and for me to tell him wonderful when I feel rotten would not have been true. What to do if cornered in a situation like that is to answer, "I don't feel well, but I am not going to receive this. This sickness was placed on Jesus and according to the Word I *am healed* and free from the curse so I'll be just fine. Thanks."

For three days I made my healing confession of faith, but I'll admit I was wondering when it was going to manifest. The Lord stopped me as I was about to take five or six vitamin C's. He said, "Healed people don't need six vitamin C's." Oh, you're right. I sure am healed — and back in the bottle went all the vitamin C's. Again I started confessing the word, but I really was feeling bad, almost into flu symptoms by now. I felt I pleased the Lord this morning, but as afternoon approached, I felt I should go to bed. (You know what they say for a cold — lots of bed rest.)

As I pulled the covers down (Oh, my, that bed looked good), again the Spirit said to me, "Healed people don't go to bed in the afternoon." (Oh, yeah, that's right.) I made that bed so fast, I thrilled myself, and right then and there every symptom left and they're not welcome back here either.

I then found Isaiah 55:11 NIV, "So is My Word that goes out from My Mouth: It will not return to me empty, but will accomplish what I desire and achieve the purpose for which I sent it."

All evening I thought on that. I determined in my mind to walk, talk, and live the Word of God. The next morning on the way to a meeting, Marilyn Hickey came on the Christian radio station. She said she felt impressed of the Lord to stop her broadcast and give a Scripture. You guessed it: Isaiah 55:11. Then she said I was not to walk in the circumstances any longer. When you stand on circumstances, you walk in unbelief. Stand on the Word of God. To do this is to walk in faith. Again, I am crying. I even pulled the car off the road. She then said, "Honey, God loves you enough to stop this broadcast." I would again remind you, God loved you enough to send His Son. Live by His Words . . . Become a man or woman of faith.

Recently I had the chance to go see a "man of faith." I found out Brother Swaggart was coming to New York. If you got your bus registered, seats were to be reserved for your group.

A church in our area got a bus together; I was thrilled to be going. We left much later than we should have for the three hour drive to New York. Since we were registered, I didn't fret. On the way up, I found out that our bus *isn't* registered, and we have no special seats waiting for us. Great woman of faith I have now become and with a wonderful confession, I start saying, "Well, we can forget about ever getting in. By the time, when we get there, it will have already started. No registration, no seats." (on and on.)

Heading to New York, it was bumper to bumper through the tunnel. I felt it was good I enjoyed the fellowship because I knew we were going to end up turning around and coming home.

As we pulled up to the front of the auditorium, there were hundreds of people out front and buses as far as the eye could see and over the loud speaker we were told they were full and if the crowd didn't disperse, the police would be called.

We unloaded and stood out front. The doors were locked with guards now at attention. We were carrying Bibles, not guns, but after all, this was the "Big Apple."

As we got back on the bus, it was all I could do to not say I told you so. A young man — a very, very new Christian — didn't want to leave. He kept saying, "I came believing." Well, from what I could see, so did all the others.

He got off the bus and went through the crowd to the guard at the door. Next thing I know this kid is going bananas on us. He told the guard that he "came believing" and the guard said he would get us in the fire escape around back — not to attract a crowd, but to bang on the door and he would get us in. All fifty?

There we were trying not to be noticed . . . just milling around, in fellowship, making our way to the fire escape.

Our believing young man banged on the door and sure enough, it opened. I didn't even need my legs, the way we stepped in, they just carried me along.

The guard counted fifty-three — three people not from our bus and group got in with us. Every one of us got a seat and at the end of the evening, those three people who ran in with us, ran up front and gave their hearts to the Lord.

I'll go believing next time!!

CHAPTER VIII
Holy Amnesia!!

Up until now I have told you of my life and the things God has done. By now you should think I am sweet, kind, and just a wonderful saint of the church. If not, please begin at page one. I am only kidding because even with Jesus Christ in my life, I have had some struggles of my own doing.

One battle I have had was with unforgiveness. I have had to learn the hard way how to forgive and to walk in love at all cost. If my sin can help you to walk in righteousness, then it will be worth sharing with you.

I had been hurt by someone very deeply and this person was, of course, a Christian. Haven't you noticed after awhile the people of the world don't really hurt you. Because they're not saved, we have a tendency to forgive them. How much more should we forgive our brothers and sisters in Christ? Much easier said than done.

I was so upset by this lady that I sat down one day and wrote a list of everything she had done to me, all the wrong I felt she committed against me. I should have offered this to God and burned it, but instead, I went to see her.

I knew the Bible said if you have aught against your brother, you go to them. Of course, I just left out the part about winning them over. I had tried and tried to get rid of my hurt and anger over all that I felt had been done against me. I just wanted to get rid of it and at this point I didn't care how.

This lady never expected what came next. I marched in on her, read my list, told her I forgave her, of course, and I love her, but I'll never fellowship with her again. Out the door I went. Because I had unloaded all this on her, I thought for sure now I would feel better and now I would again have love in my heart for her. After all, I forgave.

I couldn't get right in my heart, no matter how I tried, and I really tried. every time I would see her, all the old hurts and pain would reappear. What was wrong with me?

I felt like I was being tormented and in reality I was. Unforgiveness will torment you and I saw where Satan had an advantage over me. II Corinthians 2:10-11, "To whom ye forgive any thing, I forgive also; for if I forgave any thing, to whom I forgave it, for your sakes forgave I it in the person of Christ; Lest Satan should get an advantage of us: for we are not ignorant of his devices."

I believe with all my heart satan works hard to keep us, the Body of Christ, constantly dealing with old hurts and pains.One of his biggest devices, that tears the church apart, is unforgiveness for each other.

I am not saying you should never go to a brother who has offended you, but remember to go in love and mercy, because I am here to tell you, you reap what you sow.

That afternoon when I went with my list, I sowed a terrible seed. I showed no mercy or love at all. I was hurt, and I wanted to get even and hurt back. I knew this wasn't God's way and yet I didn't know it was Satan's way of outwitting me.

Months went by and we occasionally had fellowship with one another, even though it was strained. She may have been all right in her heart, but I wasn't and at this point I didn't think I would ever be right.

Once again the Word of God came to my rescue in Matthew 18:34-35, "And the Lord was wroth, and delivered him to the tormentors, till he should pay all that was due unto him. So likewise shall My heavenly Father do also unto you, if ye from your hearts forgive not every one his brother their trespasses."

I would pray you would read this entire parable. It's found in Matthew 18:21-35.

For the first time I saw that God had allowed me to be turned over to the tormentors because I hadn't forgiven . . . the tormentors of anger, the torment of bitterness, the torment of guilt. I wanted to forgive from my heart, but how?

I looked up the word "forgive" — it means "to give up the wish to get even." The Bible dictionary says, "the complete removal of the cause of offense *not* the offender." I realized it was my choice. It was my will. I didn't have to go on feeling this way any longer. If I pray and I forgive, that's it.

What about the memory of it? Let me say this to you. Your will *is* stronger than your memory. I thought if I forgave, I'll never remember it again. You know, forgive and forget. There is no such thing as Holy Amnesia, but I'll tell you, after you choose to forgive, you will recall the hurt, but you *will not relive* it.

We need Jesus in us to forgive through us. Our old nature wants to hold on. Forgiving the same injury over and over again is only a way of feeding yourself and your own self-pity. I know because I did it month after month until I realized I don't want to get even and if I choose to forgive, that settles it. Whenever Satan would bring it to mind, I would choose not to think about it. When he tells you you haven't really forgiven because you saw that person and you didn't turn to Jell-O, remember, he is the father of lies.

Well, I thought I had it all together now. I knew I had forgiven her, and I wasn't going to allow myself to be tormented any longer. I was going to love everyone and just show gobs and gobs of mercy.

All of a sudden, my crop came in. Remember what I said about the seeds we sow. Seems my harvest time is here. I was close to a very dear lady and we had always said to each other that if we ever do something you don't like or if I offend you, just come and tell me.

One day, while at her house for lunch, she decided to take me up on that agreement. I had hurt and offended her in a number of ways. As she kept telling me these things, one after another, I started crying and telling her how sorry I was.

I was so disappointed in myself. I thought I was really getting to be a good Christian and here I was hurting someone I loved and I hadn't even noticed. I think that bothered me more than all the things I had done that were a problem to her. I was guilty, and I knew it, but nevertheless, she had said some very hard, hard things to me, and right at that moment I remembered my list and I knew I was reaping what I had sown.

Now I was the one hurting, and I couldn't go back and make those things right. They were over, but was our friendship? Could I act like nothing happened?

I knew I needed to forgive myself and then to forgive my friend. This time I wanted total God-like forgiveness that I would let it go completely and when I was with her again, it would never enter my mind. It would be as though it never

82

happened.

This is how God does for us with our sins. Why can't we do this for each other? . . . considering that He has done this for us? I wanted to do this: be loving and forgiving.

The Lord showed me first off Proverbs 17:9, "He that covereth a transgression seeketh love; but he that repeateth a matter separateth very friends." I knew I wasn't to tell anyone of this. Many times we share more than we should. Sometimes it's even called a prayer request. I vowed before God I would not repeat this: This was the first step. Next, the Lord showed me *how to forgive*. He told me, "Don't try to understand the other person. Try instead to be understanding."

To love and to live forgiveness is to give wholehearted acceptance to others *as they are*. Forgiveness is acceptance without exception.

We can't change others; we need to allow the Holy Spirit to change us. I used to try to figure out why people would do a certain thing. No longer do I try and understand what makes them the way they are. I just accept them, and I am trying to be understanding. There is a big difference. Why not rather let error live than love die?

I want you to know what forgiveness will do for you and what it is doing for me:

> Forgiveness restores the present
> heals the future
> releases us from the past.

I chose to forgive and I chose to not repeat the matter. The very next time I saw her, I knew all was well with my soul. As for the things that I did, I am giving myself over to God. I am allowing His correction to change me.

I will not let Satan bring all those things up to me. He is the accuser of the brethren. No one said I was perfect, only forgiven.

Then came the real test. I got a letter in the mail. It seems what had happened between us was being told to a number of women. Was I going to defend myself? Don't they know there are two sides to every story. I just know the Lord didn't want me to do that. I remained silent, but it was hard. It was then the Lord brought a little poem into my life. I would pray this helps you as much as it did me.

"They're saying things that are not true: O blessed Lord, what shall I do? He answered, 'What is that to thee? Thy duty is to follow Me.'" (Anonymous)

You really can walk in love and forgiveness. I know you want to, and you will! Let's all live by I Peter 3:8-9 LB "And now this word to all of you: You should be like one big happy family, full of sympathy toward each other, loving one another with tender hearts and humble minds. Don't repay evil for evil. Don't snap back at those who say unkind things about you. Instead, pray for God's help for them, for we are to be kind to others, and God will bless us for it."

CHAPTER IX

Knife and Fork Syndrome

Here I was, walking in love and forgiveness, Jesus as Lord of my life, as long as He didn't come to the dinner table with me.

It's been over three years since I was delivered from smoking, and I didn't gain any weight for many months after that. So, I know that my problem was not related to that.

Even now I am only fifteen pounds over the charts, but I think they're fixed anyway. I found that even in a size 12 I had a terrible problem that people couldn't see, but that didn't make it any less real. I have always had a problem with food.

I have already told you why I first became heavy. It was to get my father's attention, but, even after I got it, I found I just could not stop overeating.

During those school years my best girlfriend was also heavy. We just turned each other on with all the ways we could think of to pig out.

Thanksgiving was a real wipe-out. We would have a full course meal at noon with her family and then at three, we would do it again at my house. Come seven at night we would just fall across my bed and moan. Our whole conversation was that Christmas dinner would be here before you know it, and we could do it again.

Another friend and I went to a donut shop for coffee one morning. I must have been in my senior year because we went in my car. We ordered one cream donut and coffee. We ended up eating three each in the store. I just had to have a dozen to go. I never even made it out to the parking lot. I sat there and ate the whole dozen, white powder was flying everywhere.

Once I was trying to get my jeans on. They were so tight, I had to lie on the bed, stick in my stomach to get them zipped, but then I couldn't get up! I had to roll off the bed. I was really mad — my Mom just must have shrunk them in the wash. As I tried to maneuver down the steps, I saw the tag. I had only bought these two weeks ago and they fit fine. They were brand new and had never been washed. Had someone taken in my seams as a joke? No, and I wasn't laughing now.

After I lost my weight the first time, before I got married, I just ate one meal a day, and I was able to maintain my loss. Then, after the children, I once again lost a great deal of weight. Shortly after that I was saved. No more problem, right?

I was worse than ever now because I knew it was wrong. I felt so bad that I would begin sneaking food when no one was looking. I just loved to eat alone.

I could not stay away from sweets. I would do just fine all day and as soon as the sun would go down, I would become another person almost. From cabinet to cabinet my mouth was not empty from 9 p.m. 'til bed. Then, the next day I would feel so bad I wouldn't eat all day and you guessed it, at night time I was so hungry I would just have a little . . . a little of everything that wasn't tied down or didn't move.

I decided then I would freeze all the cakes and things I couldn't handle. I had them in the house for my kids' lunches, of course.

In just one evening every time my husband wasn't looking or went out of the room for anything, I would eat a frozen Twinkie. I ate the entire box of frozen Twinkies that night. I hurt so bad I couldn't sleep on my stomach. Maybe they defrosted in there and that's why the pain? I needed help. I was driven. Food was all I could think about. Of course, I was a lifetime member in a weight group. Once, I got to my goal, and I even stayed there for a few hours.

Something was wrong. One evening I wanted an oatmeal cookie, the big ones that are individually wrapped. The kids were always in the kitchen, and I was feeling desperate. I found a pair of rubber boots in the closet that needed to go upstairs and be put away. I dropped the wrapped cookie inside the boots and headed upstairs. As I got to my room and whipped out Mr. Oatmeal, in walked my daughter. I felt caught and trapped. Was this really a Spirit-filled Christian?

Boo tried to help me and encourage me, but he knew something was wrong. I think my sneaking bothered him the most. One night, as I stood making the lunches, I was in my bathrobe, he came by and smashed all the cakes hidden in my pockets.

I wanted deliverance and help from the Lord, but I got to the point I felt ashamed to pray. When I got delivered from cigarettes, I knew I wouldn't have to smoke again, but how could I be delivered from eating?

Our church has a Women's Club dinner once a month. Honey, I never missed. Each lady brought in her specialty. I could hardly wait to get my eyes on the table. Did Bea come? She's Italian and I could count on her pasta. What about Mary? She made a mean cheese cake!

The Lord spoke to me after one of these dinners. He showed me I wasn't going there for spiritual fellowship, and the Scripture in John 6:26 is "Jesus answered them and said, Verily, Verily, I say unto you, Ye seek Me, not because ye saw the miracles, but because ye did eat of the loaves, and were filled."

I repented before God and from then on I was able to control myself at those dinners, but that was the only time I had self-control.

It was our wedding anniversary. Our neighbors, who are believers, had invited Boo and me over for a late supper — just the four of us. I couldn't wait until she got the rolls onto the table. I wanted them hot so the butter would melt in my hand. I was out of control inside myself, yet there I sat in a lady-like manner. Who would have thought I was a glutton?

As I began to dig in, the Spirit of God spoke to me and told me He wanted me to begin a fast. O.K. — I'll just eat enough now to hold me over the day I fast. Then the Spirit said, "Ten days." I beg your pardon, ten what? I didn't say a word during dinner. I think I was in a state of shock.

In the morning I was frightened and yet I wanted to obey. Maybe this would be the thing to break the bondage? I felt for sure it might kill my flesh.

Day after day, the Spirit became stronger and stronger and the flesh became weaker and weaker. On the third day I went to the Christian book store. There was a book by C.S. Lewis, called, *Help, Lord, the Devil Wants Me Fat!* When I got home with it, I found out he tells you you have to fast *ten* days to break Satan's hold over your appetite. I knew this was confirmation that it was to be ten days. I didn't think I could make it. I had never fasted that long, but I would have done anything to be free of this.

For about six months after the fast I was walking in victory. My weight was down because I had a huge weight loss on the fast, and I thought all my problems were over.

Then I fell. I ate for an entire weekend without stopping. By Monday morning I had gained nine pounds, tears, remorse, regret, yet still no self-control. Oh, God, help me!

This pattern went on for months: fast, diet, pig out. I thought I was hopeless. Don't you ever believe that! I have good news for you. No matter what your problem, Jesus is able. By the end of this chapter, you will be able to allow Him to set you free from whatever is that sin that so easily besets you.

Christmas morning my kids had saved their money and had bought me a beautiful green housecoat. As they gave it to me in love, and they were so proud because they bought it, my son Matthew said, "Mom, we got you one with two pockets for your cookies!" Oh, what was I now doing even to my kids? They don't put pockets there for cookies, although I am not sure why they are there, are you?

I was hurting and no one could help me. I would read all the Scriptures about my body being the temple of God's Spirit. I knew one fruit of the Holy Spirit in me was self-control, but in this one area I felt my tree had rotted.

In May of that year Boo came home with chocolte bars that a man was selling on the job. He had bought a dozen. Well, that night they didn't eat them, which I couldn't understand. In the morning I thought I would have just one. I ate all of them. I didn't know what to do because I couldn't go to the store and replace them. The wrappers were special because it was a fund-raiser.

That evening after supper Boo said he felt like a little piece of chocolate. I felt like something was squeezing my heart. After he opened the cabinet, seeing they were gone, he said, "Gwen, how could you let Matt and Mimi eat all that candy? Call them down here." I had to tell the truth. It was me. He looked at me and said, "You're sick." I knew he was right. I was sick, but how do I get well?

I saw an ad in the newspaper for a group starting near my home for compulsive overeaters. I had never thought about it that way. I was a compulsive overeater. I went to this meeting and for the first time I heard someone say it was an illness, a disease much like alcoholism.

They said I was sick. I said, "Amen." They said through God, I could get well and recover.

They had steps for me to follow. I needed to admit my life was unmanageable and I was powerless over food. I had to believe that God would and could restore my sanity. Make a decision to turn my will and life over to Him — I did all these things gladly.

At that group I was encouraged to stop eating sugar. They told me just for today. One day at a time. I did this. Every morning I would ask God to help me just for today. I was able, with God's help, to stop eating all the sugar products that were driving me.

Weeks started to turn into months. I was free. I had prayed for God to heal me and I was free. I didn't think of food all day long any more. I ate three meals a day. I didn't do this with will power. I did this with a surrender to Jesus each and every day.

I began to obey the voice of the Holy Spirit. I became obedient just one meal at a time. Because the sugar was gone, so was the craving. But would I stay sugar-free for the rest of my life? Could I? Was this deliverance or the easy way out?

Romans 14:14, "I know, and am persuaded by the Lord Jesus, that there is nothing unclean of itself: but to him that esteemeth any thing to be unclean, to him it is unclean."

Then I saw a warning from Jesus in Luke 21:34, "And take heed to yourselves, lest at any time your hearts be overcharged with surfeiting, and drunkenness, and cares of this life, and so that day come upon you unawares."

What in the world is surfeiting? I looked it up; it is overeating, eating until you are sick. Jesus told me to take heed; therefore, I knew I needed to be on my guard against the temptations.

Now that I realized I was a compulsive overeater, I would go to these meetings every chance that I got. We would introduce ourselves as, "Hi, I am Gwen, a compulsive overeater." I went for over six months. I had lost some weight, but the best part was my mental freedom.

About six months after joining this group I went to a church with some friends. At this service the pastor was saying how if you were an alcoholic, and Jesus heals you, then you are not an alcoholic any more. You don't go out and drink to prove your deliverance, but you don't confess you're bound either.

Well, bells went off in my head. I couldn't continue to confess I had a disease that Jesus died for. I couldn't confess week after week that I was a compulsive overeater if I believe I am healed.

I knew then that I would not be going back to that group, but I was so grateful that God put me in there so I could see what was wrong.

Yes, I had a disease, and yes, I was a compulsive overeater, but once I found that out, I could go to Jesus and be healed.

After I asked for healing and by faith received it, I had to act like a healed, delivered person. I put my faith into action. Faith without works is dead. My works were now smaller meals and eating to live, instead of living to eat.

For the next three months I continued sugar-free. Then I chose a dessert one night when I was out to eat. Would I again become crazy? Would the binges start again?

No, I am different. There are times still I don't obey or make the right choices, but I am learning Romans 14:17, "For the kingdom of God is not meat and drink; but righteousness, and peace, and joy in the Holy Ghost."

Daily I am sending out the Word of my deliverance — Isaiah 55:11. I am then acting upon the Word. I will be a doer and not a hearer only. In the spirit, I see myself thin and free. I have received God's deliverance.

Even if I give in to temptation, I am still a different person. Just the other day I made some bad choices, but not under compulsion. I then said to the Lord, "Why do I sometimes disobey? I am delivered and yet I still haven't arrived." *He spoke to me* that just because I eat the wrong things or even too much of a good thing, I am still delivered. He doesn't remove the deliverance because I fall short any more than Jesus removes our salvation because we sin.

If you want to be free, follow Matthew 6:31-33, "Therefore take no thought, saying, What shall we eat? or, What shall we drink? or, Wherewithal shall we be clothed? (For after all these things do the Gentiles seek:) for your heavenly Father knoweth that ye have need of all these things. But seek ye first the kingdom of God, and his righteousness; and all these things shall be added unto you."

I tried everything: turning from the sin of gluttony (Do this, by all means.), diets, clubs, groups, fasting, crying, and finally I got to the place where I am going to be a doer of the Word.

Your deliverance was purchased for you 2,000 years ago. Jesus came to preach deliverance to the captives and to set at liberty them that are bruised. If you feel bruised, the promise of deliverance stands today for you.

II Peter 1:4, "Whereby are given unto us exceeding great and precious promises: that by these ye might be partakers of the divine nature, having escaped the corruption that is in the world through lust."

You *have* escaped the corruption of the lust of your flesh. Therefore, since *you are* a partaker of the divine nature, you can stand on Romans 12:1, "I beseech you therefore, brethren, by the mercies of God, that ye present your bodies a living sacrifice, holy, acceptable unto God, which is your reasonable service."

Just take it one day at a time and one meal at a time. Please remember: Take no thought. Don't allow Satan to tempt you in your mind.

Fill your mind, heart, and mouth with the Word of God. Make no provision for the flesh, depend on the Holy Spirit in you to put you over, and I don't mean weight.

Jesus loves you and so do I. I'll see you at the nearest salad bar!

Philippians 4:5
Gwen

Additional books by Gwen Mouliert

Satan's Secret Weapon
– The Bite of Bitterness –

Destroy Satan's Secret Weapon
– Pain and Bitterness! –

Satan wants to keep these secrets hidden from you! The enemy is looking to establish roots of bitterness in every Christian. Don't let even tiny seeds of pain or bitterness grow into a stronghold. In this exciting book, you'll learn how to identify and destroy the venom of the viper.

You can escape from Satan's trap! Experience tremendous peace, happiness, and joy in your soul. Find new freedom! Don't let Satan deceive you. Examine key Scriptures and safeguard your heart from other people's rebellion and deceit. Renew your faith in God's ability to heal. Learn how to swing the ax of forgiveness! You'll never want to face Satan's secret weapon again! Protect yourself from all roots of bitterness. Don't give Satan any opportunity to steal from you!!! Every Christian needs God's cure for the seeds of bitterness that Satan tries to plant.

The Breastplate of the High Priest
Unlocking the Mystery of the Living Stones

Have you ever wondered what the stones in the breastplate of the High Priest represent? Since we are a royal priesthood and called by God to be living stones, we should know about the jewels of beauty that we have now become to the Lord. I was reading Ezekiel 28:13 where it talks about Lucifer before the fall: he had nine stones as his covering.

The Spirit of the Lord spoke to my heart and asked me a thought provoking question. He said, Lucifer had nine of the twelve stones on the breastplate of the high priest – what row was he missing? So began this journey to discover what each stone and row means in our lives; and as a living priesthood of believers, how we can appropriate this and shine as stones of beauty, for His glory.

CPSIA information can be obtained
at www.ICGtesting.com
Printed in the USA
FSOW02n0618121217
41824FS